Sam Bell Maxey
and the
Confederate Indians

Sam Bell Maxey
and the
Confederate Indians

John C. Waugh

Under the General Editorship of Grady McWhiney

RYAN PLACE PUBLISHERS
FORT WORTH

JH MW

Library of Congress Cataloging-in-Publication Data

Waugh, John C.
    Sam Bell Maxey and the Confederate Indians/ John C. Waugh
    p. cm.—(Civil War campaigns and commanders)
    Includes bibliographical references and index.
    ISBN 1-886661-03-0 (paperback)

    1. United States—History—(Civil War, 1861–1865—
Participation, Indian. 2. Maxey, S.B. (Samuel Bell), 1825-1895.
3. West (U.S.)—History—Civil War, 1861–1865. 4. Oklahoma—
History, Military. 5. Indians of North America—Wars—1862–1865.
    I. Title. II. Series
    E585.I53W38 1995
    973.7'464—dc20

                                   95–12958
                                        CIP

2730 Fifth Avenue
Fort Worth, Texas 76110

Printed in the United States of America

ISBN 1-886661-03-0
10 9 8 7 6 5 4 3 2 1

Book Designed by Rosenbohm Design Group

All inquiries regarding volume purchases of this book should be
addressed to Ryan Place Publishers, Inc., 4709 Colleyville Boulevard,
Suite 580, Colleyville, TX 76034-3985. Telephone inquiries may be made
by calling 817-421-9382.

A Note on the Series

Few segments of America's past excite more interest than Civil War battles and leaders. This ongoing series of brief, lively, and authoritative books–*Civil War Campaigns and Commanders*–salutes this passion with inexpensive and accurate accounts that are readable in a sitting. Each volume, separate and complete in itself, nevertheless conveys the agony, glory, death, and wreckage that defined America's greatest tragedy.

In this series, designed for Civil War enthusiasts as well as the newly recruited, emphasis is on telling good stories. Photographs and biographical sketches enhance the narrative of each book, and maps depict events as they happened. Sound history is meshed with the dramatic in a format that is just lengthy enough to inform and yet satisfy.

Grady McWhiney
General Editor

CONTENTS

CAMPAIGNS AND COMMANDERS SERIES

Map Key

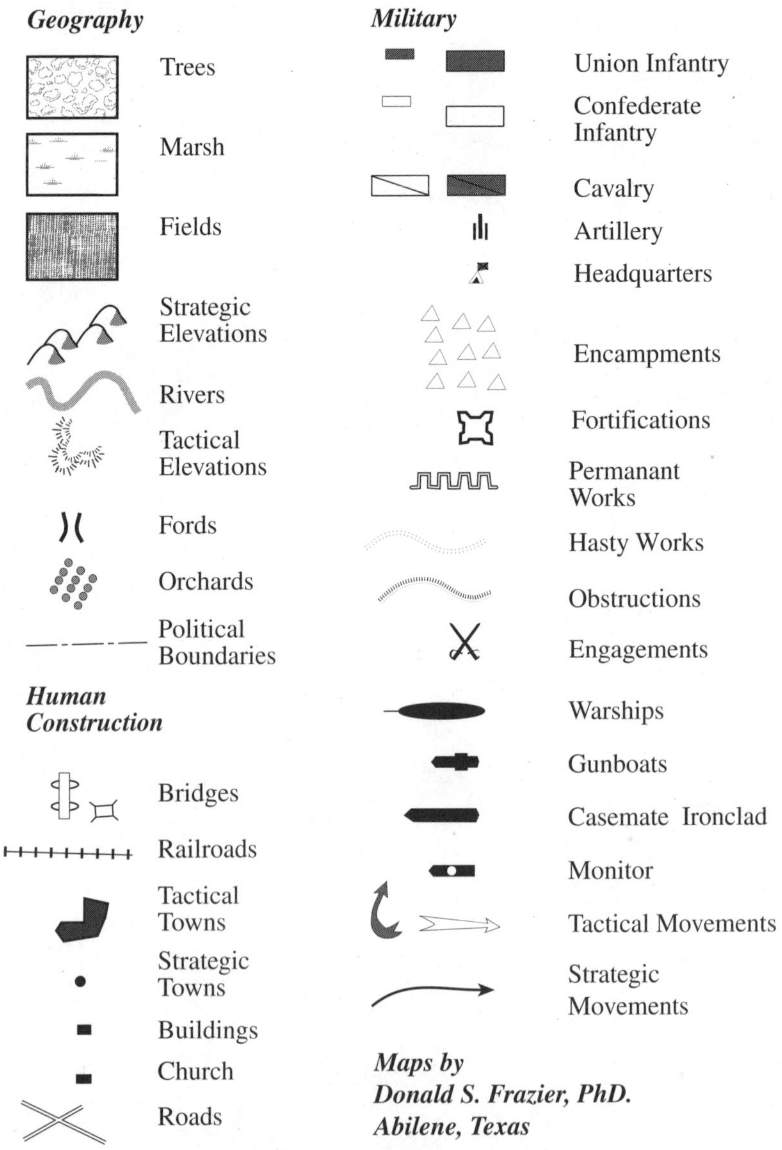

Geography

	Trees
	Marsh
	Fields
	Strategic Elevations
	Rivers
	Tactical Elevations
)(	Fords
	Orchards
—·—·—·—	Political Boundaries

Human Construction

	Bridges
+++++++++	Railroads
	Tactical Towns
•	Strategic Towns
▪	Buildings
▪	Church
✕	Roads

Military

	Union Infantry
	Confederate Infantry
	Cavalry
ılı	Artillery
	Headquarters
△ △△ △△△	Encampments
	Fortifications
⊓⊔⊓⊔	Permanant Works
	Hasty Works
	Obstructions
✗	Engagements
	Warships
	Gunboats
	Casemate Ironclad
	Monitor
	Tactical Movements
→	Strategic Movements

Maps by
Donald S. Frazier, PhD.
Abilene, Texas

MAPS

PHOTOGRAPHS

The brief biographies accompanying photographs were written by David Coffey and Grady McWhiney.

Sam Bell Maxey
and the
Confederate Indians

1
A DIFFICULT JOB FOR BEGINNERS

Sam Bell Maxey's plate was full, and what was on it was unappetizing and indigestible. He had had tough jobs before, but this one was—well, different.

He tried to describe it in a letter home from Indian Territory to his wife, Marilda, in Texas. There was a great deal to do, he wrote her, but he didn't know exactly what it all amounted to, since the duties were not well-defined.

It was an Indian problem. Maxey had hundreds of indigent Indians to feed and difficulties to settle among the tribes—not the ordinary job description for a Confederate brigadier general. Since none of the necessary supplies were available where he was, he must get them from somewhere else. And not only was he expected to defend what the Confederacy still held of Indian Territory (roughly the present state of Oklahoma), but to recover what had been lost—and all the while keep the Union army out of northern Texas.

The troops with which he must do these things were mainly Indians, and that was a problem unique to itself. It meant that his army was entirely without infantry, because infantry had to march, and Indians wouldn't march—they would only ride. It was the first army Maxey had ever heard of without an infantry—and it was his. If he succeeded in this job, he wrote Marilda, "I think I ought to be entitled to some credit."

Since it was too early for credit—it was late December 1863, and he had just come on the job—he would settle for potatoes. Please send him some potatoes, he asked Marilda,

Samuel Bell Maxey: born Kentucky 1825; graduated from the U.S. Military Academy, fifty-eighth in the class of 1846 that included George B. McClellan, Thomas J. Jackson, George E. Pickett, and other future Civil War generals; brevet 2d lieutenant 7th Infantry 1846; 2d lieutenant 8th Infantry February 1847;

transferred to 7th Infantry July 1847; participated in the Mexican War; brevetted 1st lieutenant in August 1847 for gallant conduct in the battles of Contreras and Churubusco; in 1849 he resigned his commission to study law; he and his father, who was also a lawyer, migrated to Paris, Texas, in 1857 where they practiced law in partnership; elected to the Texas senate in 1861, Maxey resigned to organize the Lamar Rifles which soon became part of the 9th Texas Infantry; that regiment, with him in command, joined General Albert Sidney Johnston's forces in Kentucky; promoted brigadier general in 1862; served in East Tennessee, at Port Hudson, and during the Vicksburg Campaign; in December 1863 made Confederate commander in Indian Territory and appointed superintendent of Indian affairs for the pro-Confederate tribes; promoted to major general by General E. Kirby Smith in 1864 but never confirmed by the president; commanded a division of dismounted cavalry in 1865; after the war he resumed his legal practice; became a U.S. senator from Texas in 1875 and served for twelve years; died in Eureka Springs, Arkansas, in 1895.

since "this is a dry old country in the eating line."

There was no doubt about it, Sam Maxey had drawn a singular assignment. There wasn't a job on either side of the war anything like this one. Few would want anything like it. "I tremble for you," his friend Samuel A. Roberts wrote from Bonham, Texas. "A great name is in store for you or you fall into the rank of failures."

Maxey's old friend from Mexican War days, Edmund Kirby (Seminole) Smith, had gotten him into this. Smith was in command of Confederate forces in the Trans-Mississippi West, a region so vast and so cut off from the rest of the Confederacy

The Trans-Mississippi

and ruled so absolutely that it was simply known as "Kirby-Smithdom."

Maxey now had a princedom in that Smithdom, the most perplexing, unpalatable barony in the entire command, the Indian Territory. Other generals before him had tried to make something of the assignment and failed. Now, at the end of 1863, for better or worse, it was Maxey's problem. He vowed he would "kick hard against the fate of my predecessors, but *stare decisis* is a hard old rule; the precedents are against me."

Maxey hadn't told Marilda the worst of it. It was an assignment to daunt the ablest of administrators. His army of Indians had largely evaporated, scattered who knows where across the Indian Territory. Discouraged by setbacks of the past year, much of the army had just drifted away, as the Indians were wont to do. One of the Indian commanders had furloughed his entire command until April Fools Day. What

Edmund Kirby Smith: born Florida 1824; graduated from the U.S. Military Academy in 1845, twenty-fifth in his class of forty-one; commissioned 2d lieutenant of infantry; earned brevets to 1st lieutenant and captain in the Mexican

War; taught mathematics at West Point from 1849 to 1852; promoted to 1st lieutenant and captain before joining the newly formed 2d Cavalry in 1855; as a major in this elite regiment, he resigned his commission in 1861 to enter Confederate service; commissioned colonel, he served on General J.E. Johnston's staff in the Shenandoah Valley; brigadier general June 1861; led troops and was wounded at First Manassas; elevated to major general in October 1861; assigned to command the Department of East Tennessee in March 1862; in conjunction with General Braxton Bragg, invaded Kentucky in the summer of 1862; after his victory at Richmond, the campaign ended after Bragg's inconclusive actions at Perryville; promoted to lieutenant general in October 1862, Smith was ordered to the Trans-Mississippi force was on hand was undisciplined, and armed, if at all, with guns of such a confusing variety that it was a nightmare just arranging an ordnance train to support it. Maxey found that his new command—he had reported for duty the day after Christmas—had no inspector general, no chief surgeon, no paymaster, indeed no pay in some cases for the past twelve months, no engineering officer, and no maps.

There were shortages of everything, beginning with uniforms. After taking an inventory, Maxey mused that Ichabod Crane could not have fashioned a suit of gray out of the entire lot. The longest and slimmest Indian alive was not long or slim enough to accommodate the largest size on hand. "The man or woman that cut these clothes," Maxey complained, "never saw a naked man. I got a pair of pants long enough, and there is a good deal of longitude about me, and they were not large enough around the waist for a ten year old boy."

Department; he assumed command there in February; the fall of Vicksburg in July 1863 left the Trans-Mississippi cut off from the rest of the Confederacy; the isolated department became known as "Kirby Smithdom" in which the general exercised virtually independent command for the balance of the war; promoted full general in February 1864; in the spring of that year the Federals launched the ambitious Red River Campaign to capture Shreveport, Louisiana; General Richard Taylor directed the repulse of Federal General N.P. Banks's approach at Mansfield and Pleasant Hill while Smith repulsed General Frederick Steele's advance in Arkansas; Taylor, angered by Smith's handling of the campaign, asked to be relieved and was later reassigned; owing to his isolation from the Confederate capital, Smith promoted several generals on his own authority, only a few of which were ever approved and confirmed by President Jefferson Davis and the Confederate Senate; with the collapse of the Confederacy, Smith surrendered the last organized Confederate force to General E.R.S. Canby at Galveston, Texas, in June 1865; fearing arrest, Smith fled to Mexico, returning to the United States several months later; after failing in business, he became president of the University of Nashville; in 1875 he joined the faculty of the University of the South at Sewanee, Tennessee. The last survivor of the eight Confederate generals of full rank, Smith died at Sewanee in 1893.

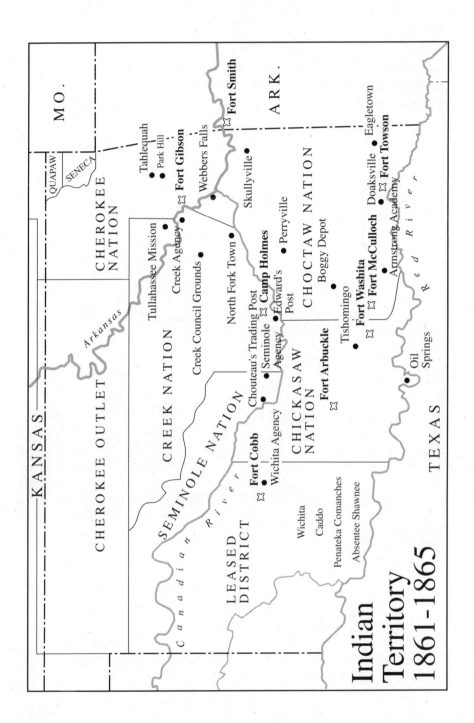

Indian Territory 1861-1865

There wasn't a tent in the entire district to sleep in, and that made it next to impossible to keep the Indians in camp in the winter weather. There were no axes or hatchets with which to build huts. Maxey was lucky that he had a bed. His bed, in fact, was one of the only points of light in the entire dismal picture. He had a pretty good one, "fodder covered," he

Jefferson Davis: born Kentucky 1808; attended Transylvania University; graduated U.S. Military Academy twenty-third in his class in 1828; appointed 2d lieutenant in the 1st Infantry in 1828; 1st lieutenant 1st Dragoons 1833; regimental adjutant 1833 to 1834; served on the Northwest frontier and in the Black Hawk War in 1832; resigned from the army in 1835 and eloped with Zachary Taylor's daughter, who died of malaria three months after their marriage; Davis settled in Mississippi as a planter; married Varina Howell and elected to Congress in 1845; resigned to participate in the Mexican War; appointed colonel 1st Mississippi Volunteer Infantry in 1846; serving under Taylor, he was wounded at Buena Vista in 1847; declined appointment to brigadier general; elected senator from Mississippi in 1847; secretary of war under President Franklin Pierce from 1853 to 1857; returned to the Senate where he served on military affairs committee until his resignation in 1861; president of the Confederate States of America from 1861 to 1865; captured following the war in Georgia, he was imprisoned at Fort Monroe for two years and never brought to trial; after failing in a number of business ventures, he was a poor man

during his later years, living at "Beauvoir," a house on the Gulf of Mexico given to him by an admirer; Mississippi would have sent him to the Senate, but he refused to ask for the Federal pardon without which it was impossible for him to take his seat; published *The Rise and Fall of the Confederate Government* in 1881; died in New Orleans in 1889. A biographer called Davis "a very engaging young man, fearless, generous, modest, with personal charm, and in friendship rashly loyal." His loyalty to the Southern cause also never faltered. But as a president he proved to be prideful, stiff, stubborn, often narrow-minded, unwilling to compromise. These qualities kept him from becoming a great chief executive.

assured Marilda, "with blankets and a very good bedstead."

Smith had warned him that this command was the most complicated in the Confederacy, and it was said that President Jefferson Davis agreed with him. Many of Maxey's friends in north Texas, those most interested in a strong Indian Territory because it was all that lay between them and a Federal invasion, advised him not to take the command. They believed no man could lift it out of the chaos it was in, and that he would only sacrifice himself and his reputation without being able to do any good.

Smith had described the command to Maxey as the *pons asinorum* of generals—very difficult for beginners. "He has sent me to the blackboard," mused Maxey, perhaps remembering the class recitations of his West Point days, "and hasn't so much as allowed me a piece of chalk to work with; only keel." And for this job he needed genuine chalk, not just a surveyor's colored marking crayon.

Maxey had come a long way since his Academy days, when he had finished fifty-eighth in the class of 1846, only one peg and a few demerits removed from classmate George Pickett, of Gettysburg fame, who had finished dead last. Maxey was a striking, commanding presence at age thirty-nine, tall and lean, with high cheek bones, a dominant Roman nose, clear blue eyes, and sandy hair. He bore himself with soldierly erectness, looking extremely good in the saddle. His long flowing beard and serious mien rather suggested a Quaker elder at a prayer meeting than a soldier at war. He spoke like a man of the cloth as well—or a lawyer, which he was, or a politician, which he aspired to be—earnestly, emphatically, and at great length.

Maxey's oratory was dignified, disarmingly plain, to the point, and logical, his arguments devastatingly thorough and persuasive. He had perfected his speaking style since leaving the army in 1849 to become a lawyer. Strong convictions, clear thinking, and a razor-like memory inherited from his verse-quoting mother, had made him a formidable advocate. It was said by a long-time friend that "one never talked to Maxey, but rather gave audience to him."

Marilda Maxey

He was cautious, patient, and deliberate by nature, his passions muted always by a strong will. This made him less than the perfect romantic match for Marilda; he signed all of his letters, even to her, "S.B. Maxey." But Maxey was also a gentleman, gallant, affable, and genial in the extreme, who seemed pleased with himself and everybody. And everybody, generally speaking, seemed pleased with him.

Over the years Maxey hadn't lost his love of sleeping in, a character flaw evident at West Point, which perhaps earned him some of his many demerits. There was a story in the Maxey family that he had once asked Thomas Jonathan Jackson—now the lost and legendary "Stonewall," but at the time Maxey's roommate at West Point—to answer early morning roll call on his behalf so he could sleep in. He was

Thomas J. Jackson: born Virginia 1824; graduated seventeenth of fifty-nine cadets in his 1846 class at the U.S. Military Academy; appointed 2d lieutenant in 3rd Artillery; participated in War with Mexico in 1847; brevetted captain for gallantry at Contreras and Churubusco and major for his conduct at Chapultepec; resigned from the U.S. Army in 1852 to accept a professorship of artillery tactics and natural philosophy at the Virginia Military Institute in Lexington, where he enforced rigid discipline, expelled several cadets, and won the hatred of many others; students called him, behind his back, "Tom Fool," "Old Blue Light," "crazy as damnation," and "the worst teach that God ever made." Jackson's first wife, Elinor Junkin, died in childbirth; a later marriage to Mary Anna Morrison produced a daughter. In 1861 Jackson joined the Confederate army; appointed colonel and then brigadier general, he won his famous nickname "Stonewall" in July at the Battle of Manassas, where General Barnard E. Bee, observing the steadiness of Jackson's very likely unsuccessful, since Jackson had a very rigid sense of duty. Maxey himself said: "I always liked to sleep. Indeed, I still feel that no gentleman transacts business before nine o'clock."

Once up, however, Maxey made the hours count. Like most West Pointers he had distinguished himself in the Mexican War. Under the direct command of this same Edmund Kirby Smith, he had helped place the gun entrenchments at Cerro Gordo, where the American army routed the Mexicans in a brilliant flanking movement in April 1847. When the army occupied the city of Mexico five months later, and the general in command, Winfield Scott, formed a city guard of five companies to keep order, Maxey was picked to command one of the five.

Virginians, shouted to his South Carolinians: "Look, men! There stands Jackson like a stone wall! Rally behind the Virginians!" Promoted to major general, Jackson began in March 1862 his brilliant Shenandoah Valley Campaign; in June he shifted his army to assist Lee in the Seven Days' Battle near Richmond; in August he fought Federal forces at Cedar Mountain, Groveton, and Second Manassas; in September, during Lee's Maryland Campaign, he captured a large Union garrison at Harper's Ferry and then rejoined Lee's army for the Battle of Sharpsburg; promoted in October to lieutenant general and commanding half of Lee's forces, Jackson repulsed a major Federal assault in December at Fredericksburg. In May 1863 he fought his last battle at Chancellorsville, where he made a spectacular flanking attack on the exposed Federal right and then rode out to locate the enemy's position; while returning in the darkness, he was mistaken for Federal cavalry and shot by his own troops. Jackson developed pneumonia and died on May 10, 1863. "I know not how to replace him," lamented Lee. Confederate Secretary of War James A. Seddon said: "Without disparagement to others, it may be safely said he has become, in the estimation of the Confederacy, emphatically 'the hero of the war.' Around him clustered with peculiar warmth their gratitude, their affections, and their hopes." As his most recent biography observed, "Stonewall Jackson ranks among the most brilliant commanders in American history. Even though his field service in the Civil War lasted but two years, his movements continued to be studied at every major military academy in

In Mexico he mapped out a master plan for the rest of his life. It called for him to resign from the army, return to Kentucky, study law, get married, move to Texas, and be elected one day to the United States Senate—roughly in that order. Up to the time he assumed command in the Indian

View of Battle of Cerro Gordo

Territory in the final days of 1863, he had accomplished the first five of those six life goals. He had even taken a first step toward the last one, having just been elected to the Texas State Senate, when the Civil War came and disrupted his program.

Maxey resigned from the army after the Mexican War, as planned, and returned to his native Pennyrile region of Kentucky. There he studied law and entered the practice with his father, Rice. In 1853 he married Marilda Cass Denton, daughter of a poor Kentucky dirt farmer and granddaughter of a sulfur-tongued Kentucky Baptist preacher. The Maxeys— father, son, and their families—moved to Texas in 1857, more or less on schedule, settling near Paris in Lamar County, on the margin of the flat northeast Texas prairie.

After Fort Sumter, Rice assumed his son's newly won seat in the state senate so Sam Bell could go off to war. Within the month, by May 1861, Maxey had raised a company of local boys for the Confederacy, called the Lamar Rifles. By September he had gone on to bigger things—command of the 9th Texas Infantry, which he took to join Albert Sydney Johnston's Confederate army in Kentucky. By March 1862 he was a brigadier general, soon to be in charge of organizing Confederate forces around Chattanooga. He was making his mark mainly as an administrator—and a very good one. A year later, in July 1863, he was with Joseph E. Johnston's army in Mississippi, watching helplessly as Vicksburg fell to Ulysses S. Grant. Disgusted, Maxey asked to be transferred to Kirby-Smithdom across the river, and in December Smith assigned him to the Indian Territory and told him to do something, for God's sake, about the Confederate Indians.

Smith couldn't have made a better choice. This was coming home for Maxey. It was his country. Paris, Texas, which he had left to go to war, was just across the border from the Indian Territory. Over the years he had come to know that territory well. As he himself had said, he had "very closely studied my subject." Also over the years he had proved a gifted administrator, full of drive and ability. He knew how to talk, and the Indians liked good talkers. He could be counted on to handle the situation with understanding, sensitivity, and tact.

Area of Operations 1864

Fort Scott

KANSAS

QUAPAW

MO.

SENECA

CHEROKEE
OUTLET

Arkansas

Cabin Creek
(Sept. 19, 1864)

CHEROKEE
NATION

Tahlequah

Park Hill

Tullahassee Mission

CREEK NATION

Creek Agency

Fort Gibson

Creek Council Grounds

Webbers Falls

Fort
Smith

SEMINOLE
NATION

North Fork Town

J. R. Williams captured
(June 15, 1864)

Skullyville

Canadian

Edward's
Post

Perryville

ARK

CHOCTAW NATION

Fort Arbuckle

Boggy Depot

Tishomingo

CHICKASAW
NATION

Fort Washita

Armstrong
Academy

Doaksville

Eagletown

Fort Towson

Oil
Springs

Red   River

TEXAS

If order could be resurrected from chaos, Smith believed Maxey could probably do it as well as anybody.

Maxey had a clearer idea of what needed to be done than he let on to Marilda. It was essential that the Federal army be kept out of north Texas. Maxey could put his whole heart in that part of the job, because north Texas was his home and the source of all his supplies. If possible, the Union army must be driven from the Indian Territory and out of striking range of the Lone Star State. The Federal army's presence had already made much of the territory into a no man's land and turned thousands of Indians into homeless refugees, whom Maxey now had to feed. The Indian Confederate soldiers must be reorganized and battles fought. The job would tax all of Maxey's administrative and military skills.

The stakes were high. In Maxey's opinion, loss of the Indian Territory would be the most pestilential plague that could be visited on the Trans-Mississippi Department. In his mind it would work a more permanent injury than the loss of any state in the Confederacy. States can be recovered; the Indian Territory, once lost, could never be. Whites when exiled find friends among their own race. Indians have nowhere to go. "Let the enemy once occupy the country to Red River and the Indians give way to despair," Maxey predicted. Nor would the ruin stop there; it would spread into Texas, a contingency to be avoided at whatever price.

Therefore Maxey never stopped lobbying Smith to spare no pain or effort to maintain the treaties with the Indians and keep every pledge made to them. "The utter folly and shortsightedness of neglecting so great an interest, or ever endangering it in any way," Maxey wrote, "is too important to a man of sense to need elaboration."

Besides, there was another important, far more personal matter at stake. "If I fail to hold this country," Maxey admitted candidly to Smith, "my reputation will be damned."

2

INDIAN COUNTRY

The Indians Maxey was commanding were not the same sort as those the army had hunted and fought on the western frontier in the years before the war. These were the Indians of the Five Civilized Tribes—Cherokees, Creeks, Choctaws, Chickasaws, and Seminoles. They were so civilized they owned slaves. For that and other reasons they were allied with the Confederacy and not the Union.

The U.S. government had run these five Indian tribes out of their ancestral homes in the southeast over the Trail of Tears and relocated them in Indian Territory in the 1830s. Even before that they had been well in advance of most other North American Indian tribes. The Cherokees, the largest of the five nations, published the first volume of laws ever by an American Indian government in 1821, and the first Indian newspaper in 1828. By the eve of the Civil War, the Cherokees owned 2,504 black slaves. The Choctaws owned 2,297, the Creeks 1,651, and the Chickasaws 917. Only the Seminoles had no slaves.

When the war came the Indians, like everybody else, had to choose sides. The geographical location of the Indian Territory made neutrality impossible. From the very beginning the Choctaws and the Chickasaws had no problem; they were Confederates through and through. Most of the Creeks and Seminoles were as well. Only the Cherokees, 21,000 in number, the biggest of the Five Civilized Tribes, were seriously divided. But they had been divided for years over many things, warring violently among themselves. Some of them, the "least in wealth and intelligence" in Maxey's view, followed their principal chief, that "traitor and deserter John Ross," into exile in Kansas. The rest of the Cherokees under "their chivalrous old chief Stand Watie," stayed to fight for the Confederacy and had remained "as true as the needle to the North Star." It was not difficult to tell where Maxey stood on these matters.

The Confederacy moved swiftly to bond the Indians to their cause after Fort Sumter. Jefferson Davis sent an adroit emissary, Albert Pike, to negotiate treaties and pry the tribes loose from the Federal protectorate. Pike was a perfect choice, a heavyweight in every sense, a formidable 300-pound mountain of flesh with a profuse and flowing patriarchal beard capped by a Medusa-like head of cascading locks. This massive exterior, impressive enough, housed a scholar of tact and sensitivity that was even more impressive. Pike understood Indians, spoke their languages, and could also negotiate with them in French, Spanish, Greek, Latin, or Sanskrit if they preferred.

He came up from Arkansas, and before the end of 1861 he had all of the five nations locked in by treaty to the Confederacy. The Indians began to organize for the warpath—into regiments and battalions. They were to fight as separate Indian units under their own chosen commanders. Two Cherokee mounted rifle regiments were organized under John Drew and Stand Watie. Douglas H. Cooper, a white Indian agent, mustered a regiment of Choctaws and Chickasaws. The Creeks organized separately under two of their leaders, the McIntosh brothers—Daniel and Chilly. The Seminoles were collected into a small battalion under their chief, John Jumper. By October, four regiments, three battalions, and a number of

Albert Pike: born Massachusetts 1809; when plans to attend Harvard fell through, he moved to Arkansas; edited a newspaper in Little Rock and practiced law; as a

lawyer, he pursued Indian grievances in Federal courts; served in the Mexican War; a highly-regarded author and poet, Pike became a prominent land owner in Arkansas; at the outbreak of the Civil War he was sent by the Confederate government to negotiate alliances with the Cherokee, Chickasaw, Choctaw, Creek, and Seminole Nations; brigadier general August 1861; headed the Department of Indian Territory; led Indian troops in the Battle of Elkhorn Tavern, Arkansas, in March 1862, but drew blame for his command's poor conduct during the battle; subsequent differences with General Thomas C. Hindman, commander of the Trans-Mississippi Department, and accusations of atrocities committed by Pike's Indian troops resulted in Pike's resignation in July 1862; following accusations of insanity and disloyalty leveled by General Douglas Cooper, Pike's resignation was accepted in November; he passed the remainder of the war in Arkansas and Texas, but a distrusted figure, he saw no further duty; after the war he moved to Washington, D.C., where he resumed his writing; a devoted Freemason, he wrote *The Morals and Dogma of the Ancient and Accepted Scottish Rite* (1872); an earlier work, *Prose and Poems Written in the Western Country* (1834) was widely praised. General Pike died at Washington in 1891.

independent companies had been organized. Pike himself had been named to overall command of this emerging army of Indians, and the Confederacy began to arm and equip them as best it could.

Also by October, the Federals, whose hold on the Indian Territory had been tenuous to begin with, had been driven into Kansas with their Indian allies—mostly non-Confederate Cherokees. The Confederates had quickly occupied the three forts then existing in the interior of the Indian Territory. Maxey, in fact, had come up with his Lamar Rifles as part of the liberating force.

Fort Washita, the first of these forts, erected in pre-Mexican War days by Zachary Taylor, was in the southeastern corner of the Chickasaw Nation. Fort Arbuckle, also in Chickasaw country, was situated sixty miles to the northwest of Washita. Fort Cobb, the third fort, was one hundred miles to the northwest of Arbuckle, in what was called the Leased District, the home of various independent Indian tribes. Boggy Depot in the Choctaw Nation became the main commissary station and staging ground of the Confederate forces in Indian Territory. A public well stood in the middle of Boggy Depot, near a tall pole topped by a Confederate flag, around which the Indian soldiers galloped on ponies and sang war songs. The Confederates also took control of two critical strongholds on the Arkansas River to the northeast—Forts Smith and Gibson.

With all of these acquisitions the Confederates started the war firmly in control of the Indian Territory. But that hadn't lasted. The Federal government, bent on reclaiming the territory, had mounted two invasions out of Kansas since 1862. The first of these had failed. The second in 1863, however, had rolled the Confederates back below the Arkansas River and stripped them of Forts Smith and Gibson. Half of the Indian Territory, including all of the Cherokee Nation, was seized. Nearly sixteen thousand Confederate Indians were

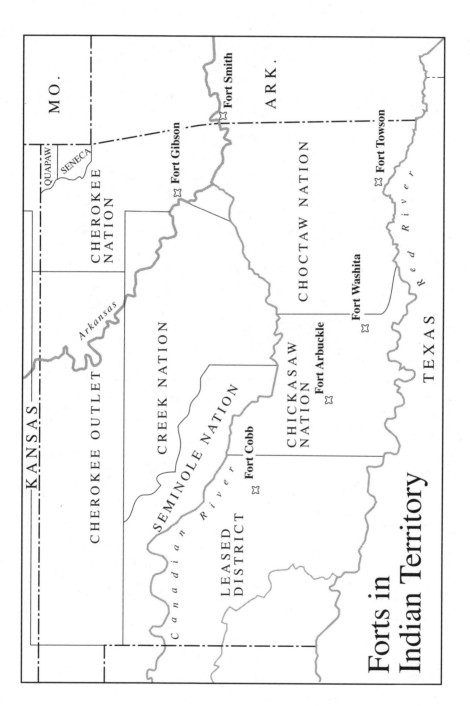

Forts in
Indian Territory

turned into homeless refugees. A loss at the battle at Honey Springs in July 1863, and other Confederate setbacks through the fall, had put Confederate fortunes on a downward slide and opened a serious rift in Confederate-Indian relations. The hard-pressed Rebel government wasn't living up to its treaty obligations and there was chaos everywhere.

That is how Maxey found things in December 1863 when he took on this troubled command. His army was scattered, demoralized, disorganized, and driven back to the Red River where nature offered no logical line of defense; the refugees must be fed; and the Confederate-Indian alliance was in shambles.

Maxey set up his headquarters at Fort Towson on the Red River in Choctaw country, an abandoned Federal fort with only a hospital and one barracks building still standing, and took an inventory. On paper he had an impressive force—an army of 8,875 men. But in the winter camps at Boggy Depot and Doaksville he could count only 2,236 troops present. The Indian Brigade, allegedly the most substantial organization in the territory, now under the over-all command of the ex-Indian agent, Douglas Cooper, had 659 present for duty and 5,585 absent. Maxey also had a thousand white troops at his disposal under Colonel Richard M. Gano, but it was bitterly split by personnel problems and wholesale desertions.

It was enough to give a man an incurable headache. By the end of January 1864 Maxey was feeling keen to break the grip of the "infernal office drudgery." He longed for a decent-sized fight, to give him the will and the energy to keep going.

Besides, there was trouble at home in Paris, adding to his distractions. Marilda had been feeling ill, depressed, and suicidal. She had written Maxey that nobody cared if she lived or died. Not so, he hastily reassured her. "Don't talk and feel so gloomily as you say in your letter. I don't know how you can say no one would miss you. Perhaps I have not shown that interest and love for you and your welfare that I ought to. I am full of fault, speak roughly sometimes, when I ought not, but God knows you would at least leave one lonely and sad."

While a healthier, happier wife was in Maxey's immediate future, a decent-sized fight wasn't. He still had more hard, demanding administrative work to do. He must attend an important meeting of the Grand Council of the United Indian Nations, the governing body of the five Confederate tribes, at the Armstrong Academy in February. It was an important meeting, critical to the future of the alliance. It would be Maxey's first exposure to the leaders of the Indian nations and he had to do well. A good first impression would restore the confidence of the Indians in the Confederacy; a bad impression would be disastrous. Smith wrote approving his plans to attend, urging him to "do all in your power to cheer and encourage them."

They would need more than cheer and encouragement. Maxey knew Indians, and he knew that with Indians, immediately behind despondency generally followed bleak despair. The Confederacy had won Indian allegiance in 1861 in part because Pike had offered them political integrity, political equality, and bona fide protection. The various treaties had recognized the Indian land rights and existing territorial limits, and the Confederacy had backed the treaties with pledges to keep the Indian soldiers well supplied with guns and equipment.

As Maxey prepared to leave for the meeting at the Armstrong Academy, the Confederacy was living up to very few of these obligations. It was a good thing he had a way with words; he had some explaining to do.

The Armstrong Academy had been an Indian boys' school in more quiet times. But in war it was the capital of the Choctaw Nation, the capital of the Confederacy in Indian Territory, and a troop concentration center. It was where the Grand Council met, and the Council was meeting this February to reassess the alliance and to decide the next step. The new commander of the Indian Territory had been invited to speak.

Calling up all of his lawyer's eloquence, Maxey apologized for the Confederacy's inability to meet many of its treaty obligations in the past year, promised that those obligations would be kept, and pledged victory in the year ahead. It was a lawyer-like job, well-received. Maxey's sincerity and enthusiasm came through, helped by the timely arrival of a message from Jefferson Davis apologizing for not yet delivering the promised annual annuity.

A "noble address," said one of the councilmen of Maxey's oration. A written copy was requested for closer scrutiny and interpretation. It had been enough to convince the Indians, even without a further reading, to stick with the Confederacy. "I am convinced that the effect was beneficial," Maxey wrote the Confederate Commissioner of Indian Affairs. Even Douglas Cooper, commander of the Indian brigade under Maxey, who wanted Maxey's job and would give him no end of trouble in the coming months, thought it "had an excellent effect."

By mid-February Maxey was able to tell Smith that he was "beginning to see my way." If only he could get guns. That was his biggest problem. The Indians had been promised guns under the treaty and they hadn't been forthcoming. That and the fact that they had not received their annuity payment were the two things that most severely shook Indian confidence in the Confederacy. Maxey had been assured by Smith that three thousand guns were, in effect, on the way. But they hadn't arrived.

"The great trouble, and the one about which I have more anxiety than all others," Maxey wrote Marilda, "is arms. Oh for 5,000 good guns.... I have the promise, but when will it be fulfilled?" Perhaps Maxey would be reduced to practice something his West Point roommate, Stonewall Jackson, had preached in his stunning Shenandoah Valley campaign in the late spring of 1862: "We must, under Divine blessing, rely upon the bayonet when fire-arms cannot be furnished."

Maxey's ordnance officer told him that many of the men were not as well armed "as the wild Indian with his tomahawk and war club." Even Maxey's white troops were ill equipped. The Texas Partisan Rangers in Richard Gano's brigade were armed only with shotguns, squirrel rifles, and one mammoth Belgium musket.

This distressing lack of arms was one of the first things Captain R.W. Lee, Maxey's newly appointed inspector general, noticed. "Obtain arms for them, general," he said, "and their now gloomy faces will grow bright, and their cheerful voices will again soon ring around their now deserted homes."

The guns would never come. In September, nine months after taking command, Maxey was still pleading for them in letters to Smith. "The cry for arms," he wrote him on September 12, "is serious." It wasn't that Smith didn't want to give the Indians guns; he simply didn't have any to give. It was the twilight of the Confederacy and everything was hard to come by.

Not only did Maxey's new command lack guns; it had that other bizarre problem of Indian warfare—no infantry. "Cavalry and Artillery without infantry make a singular sort of army," Maxey admitted. He had what was known in any other army as a cavalry command, pure and simple. A more woebegone cavalry there could never be, uniformed for the most part in shredded rags, armed with antique firearms, and riding decrepit horses.

Maxey knew that what you got with a cavalry command was "a running fight as usual." But there was nothing to do but to adjust. There was no self-respecting Indian alive, no matter how shabbily dressed, inadequately armed, or ill mounted, who would fight on foot.

"Constantly watching for weak places or insufficiently protected interests where we might run in, deliver a damaging blow and fly quickly to the cover of our base," explained one of them, was the Indian way—all, of course, on horseback. That was the way they were; it suited their character.

3

NOT YOUR ORDINARY FIGHTER

Highly unsuited to the hit-and-run Indian character was discipline of any sort. Orders to Indians, one officer put it simply, "have as little effect as 'Mexican pronunciamentos' with as little power vested in the comdr to enforce them." This was even true for Douglas Cooper, the officer in overall field command of the Indian troops under Maxey, who was the white man the Indians most respected. He had no more command over them, except the influence he wielded from long association with and universal kindness to them, than if he was not their general at all.

Not even the greatest of the Indian commanders under Cooper, the Cherokee colonel, Stand Watie, could do anything with them—except fight them as a band of independent-minded cohorts. But he did that very well. Watie had the reputation as one of the finest guerrilla fighters on either side of the war. Maxey admired him, and called him "that old war chief Watie." He wrote Smith wistfully that he wished some white commanders had as much energy.

Watie was a swart little man with legs custom-bowed to wrap around the sides of his horse. In battle he wore a black plantation coat, grey flannel trousers, and knee-high riding boots. On his head over a long flowing mane of black hair he

Stand Watie: born Cherokee Nation (Georgia) 1806; attended mission school; became a planter and published a Cherokee newspaper; a leading member of the faction that supported Cherokee resettlement in the West; signed the Treaty of Echota in 1835 that led to the Cherokee removal to Indian Territory (Oklahoma) and bitterly divided the Cherokee Nation—the other leaders of the pro-removal faction were all killed; relocated to Indian Territory; a slaveowner, he organized the Knights of the Golden Circle; at the outset of the Civil War the division among Cherokees left Watie the leader of a minority favoring the Confederacy; he raised a regiment of Cherokees for Confederate service and in July 1861 became colonel of the Cherokee Mounted Rifles; fought at Wilson's Creek, Missouri, in August and further helped secure the Confederacy's hold on the Indian Territory in the Battle of Chustenahlah; led his Indian troops in the Battle of Elkhorn Tavern, Arkansas, in March 1862; elected principal chief of the Confederate Cherokees in August; over the next three years Watie's command engaged in numerous raids, small actions, and skirmishes in the Indian Territory and surrounding areas; commissioned brigadier general in May 1864 and given command of an Indian brigade; finally surrendered in June 1865–the last Confederate  general to do so; after the war he engaged in planting and pursued business interests in the Indian Territory; he died at his home in 1871. Recognized for his personal bravery and loyalty to the Confederacy, General Watie was the only Indian to become a general officer during the war. His Indian troops proved to be capable raiders and fought effectively in spontaneous actions; they were, however, poorly suited for pitched battle.

wore a black slouch hat to shield his face and eyes from the beating sun, wind, and rain. The old warrior took pride in being an Indian. He had named one of his daughters Minnehaha, Laughing Water, after the dark-eyed beauty of poet Henry Wadsworth Longfellow's popular epic Indian hymn, *The Song of Hiawatha.*

He was a man of great natural ability, who spoke abruptly or not at all. He had been a fixture in the divided Cherokee leadership for three decades and had never been an orator even in his native tongue. But he wrote with ease and eloquence, characteristic of Indians. His birth name, "Takertawker," meant "to stand firm; immovable," which he had shortened to Stand. His last name, Oowatie, also got pruned back in school simply to Watie. It was said of him that no one ever rose to a place of such importance who had less to say.

Watie was not as rigid a disciplinarian as Maxey felt he ought to be, was nothing of a tactician, and did not keep his men together at all well. But Maxey saw that he had "a comprehensive view of the great principles involved in this war,....a well balanced and well formed mind—more brain than nine tenths of the white race—energy of fixedness of purpose—unquestioned patriotism and courage, and the confidence not only of his brigade but of the entire Indian people, and a thorough knowledge of the country and of Indian character." Watie never asked any of his men to do anything he wouldn't do himself, and he never ordered a charge he didn't lead. That was good enough for Maxey.

There wasn't just Watie, although he was the best of the Indian commanders. The finest Indian troops in the territory as far as Maxey was concerned were the Choctaws and Chickasaws. Their commander, Tandy Walker, was "a brave man, of good mind and well informed." The Seminole chief, John Jumper, was a dignified mountain of a man and a fluent speaker, but wholly unable to read or write. And there were the two Creek brothers, the McIntoshes, Daniel with the long hair and goatee, and the toothless but eloquent Chilly. Like Watie, these other Indian commanders, if not able to discipline their men, were quite capable of inspiring them. George Washington Grayson, a young Creek captain, heard Chilly McIntosh, who was also a Baptist preacher, deliver the finest war speech he ever heard. "When you first saw the light," Chilly sermonized as they waited for the battle of Honey Springs to begin, "it was said of you 'a man child is born.' You must prove today whether or not this saying of you was true.

Douglas H. Cooper: born Mississippi 1815; attended the University of Virginia, 1832–1834; not graduating, he returned to Mississippi to engage in planting;

during the Mexican War he served under his close friend Jefferson Davis in the 1st Mississippi Rifles; in 1853 he gained a Federal appointment as Indian agent to the Choctaw Nation; at the outbreak of the Civil War he was commissioned by the Confederate government to cultivate alliances with the Cherokee, Chickasaw, Choctaw, Creek, and Seminole Nations; became colonel of the 1st Choctaw and Chickasaw Mounted Rifles; with his regiment, he patrolled the Indian Territory and participated in the fighting at Chustenahlah in December 1861; in 1862 he was engaged at Elkhorn Tavern and Newtonia, Arkansas, after which he openly criticized the mental fitness and loyalty of General Albert Pike; brigadier general 1863; fought at Honey Springs, Indian Territory, in July 1863; led an Indian brigade in General Sterling Price's 1864 Missouri invasion; in February 1865, over the objection of General E. Kirby Smith, Cooper was named commander of the District of Indian Territory and superintendent of Indian Affairs, replacing General Samuel Bell Maxey; following the war he represented the Chickasaws and Choctaws in legal actions against the United States. General Cooper died in the Chickasaw Nation in 1879.

The sun that hangs over our heads has no death, no end of days. It will continue indefinitely to rise and set; but with you it is different. Man must die sometime, and since he must die, he can find no nobler death than that which overtakes him while fighting for his home, his fires and his country." The speech was followed shortly by orders to retire—an anticlimactic development—but it was the thought that counted.

It was plain to Maxey that what these Indians urgently needed was to be reorganized. His idea was to reshape them into two cohesive brigades, one under the command of Colonel Watie, the other under some other Indian commander to be named, and both under the direct field command of Douglas Cooper.

Cooper was not your ordinary subordinate. In the first place being subordinate at all galled him. He had wanted Maxey's job, and everybody knew it. He had wanted the job when it belonged to Pike, and he had wanted it when it belonged to Pike's successor, Brigadier General William Steele. In time he managed to drive both of those men out of the Indian Territory, and when Smith named yet another pretender to the job— Maxey—it was nearly more than Cooper could stand. Cooper was clearly one of Maxey's biggest problems.

Maxey knew from the start that he was in for it from Cooper. He had hardly taken up his new duties when he received a letter from Albert Pike. "I do not want to see you, also demolished by being in command of the Indian Territory," Pike wrote him. "You will have to leave Gen'l Cooper in almost uncontrolled command of the Indians," he warned, "or you will have trouble." Pike offered other advice as well, and said "I make these suggestions because I have been through the mill, and know how grain is crushed between the upper and nether mill stones."

Cooper, then, went with the territory—he had to be put up with and accommodated, and not much else could be done about it. He considered the job of commander of Indian Territory to be rightfully his, no matter who occupied it. Maxey had to move carefully, because Cooper also had clout. For one thing, he had inordinate influence with Jefferson Davis, a fellow Mississippian. Cooper had been one of Colonel Davis's lieutenants in the Mexican War, and as Secretary of War under Franklin Pierce, Davis had gotten Cooper the job at the Choctaw agency. Cooper wouldn't hesitate to use this important connection to get what he wanted.

In addition, Cooper had almost hypnotic sway over the Indians, particularly the Choctaws and Chickasaws. He was gifted with a remarkable understanding of the problems and

William Steele: born New York 1819; graduated U.S. Military Academy in 1840, thirty-first in his class of forty-two; commissioned 2d lieutenant and assigned to dragoons; fought in the Seminole wars; brevetted for gallantry in the Mexican War; promoted to 1st lieutenant; captain 2d Dragoons 1851; served on the frontier, mainly in Texas, where he married into a Texas family; resigned his commission in 1861 to enter Confederate service; appointed colonel 7th Texas Cavalry; participated in General Henry Hopkins Sibley's ill-fated New Mexico Expedition; brigadier general September 1862; commanded the Department of Indian Territory for most of 1863, being superseded by General Samuel Bell Maxey in December; briefly served in Galveston before joining General Richard Taylor's command in opposition to General N.P. Banks's 1864 Red River Campaign; led a cavalry brigade with distinction at Mansfield, Pleasant Hill, and Blair's Landing; temporarily assumed command of General Thomas Green's cavalry Division following that officer's death, but was quickly superseded by General John Wharton; after the war General Steele was a commission merchant in San Antonio and held several public offices, including adjutant general of the state of Texas in which he oversaw the reorganization of the Texas Rangers. He died at San Antonio in 1885.

needs of the Choctaw people and an empathy with them. There was nothing he wouldn't do for them. Over the years he had proved their unfailing friend, respectful of their leaders and respected by them. When in 1856 he was named agent to the Chickasaws as well, he had the same affect on them. The Choctaws named a county in their territory for him, and the Chickasaws made him a Chickasaw; they both loved him.

Cooper was a passionate pro-states, pro-slavery southerner through and through. He credited the rapid advancement of the Indians in the territory to slavery. When the Civil War began, he was authorized by the Confederate secretary of war to raise a mounted regiment of Choctaws and Chickasaws and to be their commander. He was soon a colonel, then a brigadier general. With his considerable political clout he had rid the territory of Albert Pike, and very quickly of William Steele, whose lack of acquaintance with the people and the topography disgusted him.

Steele in particular had no chance against this well-connected and consummate propagandist. In October 1863, Richmond was flooded with petitions from the Indians to dump Steele, make the Indian Territory a separate command, and put Cooper in charge. Unable to take that kind of heat, Steele resigned. The way seemed clear at last for Cooper.

Smith, however, was a serious stumbling block. He did not share Davis's affection and regard for Cooper. The man had rather more ambition than he had military talent as far as Smith, a West Pointer, could see. And since this was Kirby-Smithdom, not Jefferson-Davisdom, Smith brought in Maxey instead. He told Cooper that although he would continue as the commander of the Indian troops in the field—a delicate intermediate position between Maxey and the Indians—he would still be subject to Maxey's orders. This was more than Cooper could endure. He appealed again to his friend Davis, and orders were on the way to Shreveport from Richmond by late July ordering Smith to give command of the Indian Territory to Cooper. When the orders arrived, Smith simply ignored them.

Now, when Maxey wanted to reorganize the Indians into two brigades, he found himself running further afoul of Cooper. Cooper wanted three Indian brigades, not two—a brigade of Cherokees under Watie, a brigade of Creeks and Seminoles under Colonel Daniel McIntosh, and a brigade of Choctaws and Chickasaws under Colonel Tandy Walker. Although Cooper preferred the three-brigade arrangement partly because it better satisfied his own personal ambitions, there was also a good reason for it. He argued correctly that three brigades would more likely satisfy the Indians themselves, who wished to fight as nations, and resisted any arrangement that infringed on their separate tribal identities. They had allied themselves with the Confederacy as nations and it was as nations that they wished to fight. Choctaws and Chickasaws might serve harmoniously in the same brigade. Creeks and Seminoles might mesh peaceably. But there was no brigade on earth big enough to hold Choctaws and Cherokees at the same time; it would be a toss-up whether they would fight the Yankees or each other.

Maxey understood these alliances and animosities as well as Cooper, and he was flexible. Cooper favored three brigades, the Indians themselves favored three, and Davis had decreed three. So three it would be, and it didn't matter much to Maxey as long as it got done.

Getting it done was Maxey's bottom line in everything. It was what made him such an able administrator. It was what made him agreeable now to any combination that made getting it done happen. "I have never been troubled in my life with 'red tape-ism,'" he wrote his fellow general and Texan, Henry McCulloch.

"Common sense and the good of the service control my

actions." His great end and aim, he said, was "to give my bleeding country every energy of mind and body. Outside of that I have no ambition—no vengeance to appease, no father, son, or brother or kin to promote."

Maxey's philosophy of battle, although he had not been in many of them, was just as pragmatic: "to meet the enemy on his advance and contest every foot of ground." In his mind it was the true and only way to fight.

While reckless disregard of duty disgusted him and he wouldn't tolerate it in his command, he treated right-acting

Henry E. McCulloch: born Tennessee 1816; moved to Texas in 1837; sheriff of Gonzales County, Texas; fought in several actions against Indians; commanded a company of Texas Rangers in the Mexican War; elected to the state legislature in

1853 and to the state senate two years later; appointed U.S. marshal for the eastern district of Texas in 1859; upon the secession of Texas, he received a Confederate commission as colonel; organized the 1st Texas Mounted Rifles to seize U.S. posts on the northwest Texas frontier and to protect the frontier from Indian attacks; briefly commanded the Confederate Department of Texas in 1861; afterward he headed a succession of districts and sub-districts in Texas; he was instrumental in assembling and forwarding troops for service outside the state; brigadier general 1862; in his only major combat action, McCulloch led a brigade at Milliken's Bend during the Vicksburg Campaign of 1863; his poor showing in handling a large body of troops brought a swift return to Texas; although he later commanded the important Northern Sub-district of Texas, his duties remained largely administrative; after the war he engaged in farming and ranching in Guadalupe County and was the superintendent of the Texas Asylum for the Deaf and Dumb; he died at Rockport, Texas, in 1895. Although he fared poorly as a combat commander, General McCulloch was a talented and useful administrator. His brother, Confederate General Ben McCulloch, was killed at Elkhorn Tavern, Arkansas, in 1862.

men under him with unfailing fairness, sensitivity, consideration, and tact. Kindness has a wonderful influence, Maxey believed, but beneath the glove of silk should curl the fist of iron. He considered an army "a school for grown boys on a large scale, where perfect firmness (without harshness) tempered by kindness and sometimes mercy should preside." It would preside in his army of Indians if he had his way.

The Indians liked this big-boned Texan, and that was saying a lot. They hadn't much liked any Texan since Sam Houston. Maxey knew how to treat them. He was a propagandist of rare skill and they liked the things he was cranking out on his printing press at Fort Towson. Everything he issued had the same general message, be it overt or subliminal—that no effort be spared to hold the Indian country. They liked that. They also liked the way he complimented and praised them, calling them "the good and true men of the Indian Territory."

They also liked his position on racial issues. In line with his basic pragmatism, Maxey didn't care whether a man was red or white or any other color. Confederate law recognized no distinctions between Indian and white officers of the same rank, and he held emphatically to that principle. No race or color line would be drawn in assessing the relative rank of officers in his command. If an Indian deserved to be a general, he would be a general, and in fact from the beginning Maxey worked to get Watie promoted to that rank.

This attitude didn't sit well with some of Maxey's white officers. One of them, Colonel Charles DeMorse, of Gano's brigade, protested bitterly that "if...it is expected that the white man will be subordinated to the Indian, I ask respectfully to be immediately relieved from duty in this district." DeMorse could relax. Maxey didn't intend to put white troops under Indian command, but neither would he hesitate to promote Indians to rank coequal with their white counterparts.

Maxey had far bigger problems than racial bigotry to deal

Union Indian soldiers at rest.

with. He had a refugee problem he had inherited and must now
somehow solve. The Red River was lined as far as his eye could
see with Confederate Indian refugees—thousands of them,
destitute, hungry, suffering, and homeless. These were Indians
who had owned things in Indian Territory—homes, grain, hides,
horses, oxen, cattle, salt, lead, and slaves. But in the Federal
invasion of the past terrible summer, two thirds of the Indian
Territory had been stripped from Confederate hands and turned
into a desolated middle ground terrorized by bands of white
outlaws and revenge-seeking Federal Indians. Scarcely a
Confederate household remained in the occupied region.

The refugees, said Stand Watie, whose own wife, Sarah, was
among them, had been "only too glad to escape with their lives."
In August 1863 Watie had written the Confederate
commissioner of Indian affairs in Richmond: "I cannot under-
stand the soundness of the policy which allows a vastly inferior
force of the enemy to ravage the land with impunity." Watie was
very likely more concerned for others of his people than for his
wife. As she once said of herself, "It is a saying that Mrs. Watie
will get along where others will sink."

Now these others lined the banks of the Red River and were
flooding into north Texas. They had to be fed. The numbers were
staggering: nearly 5,000 Creeks, 3,000 Cherokees, 5,000
Choctaws, more than a thousand Seminoles, nearly a thousand
Chickasaws, and another thousand Reserve Indians and
Osages—about 16,000 in all, homeless, destitute, and
dependent on the Confederate government. "These great
privations," several of the Indian leaders wrote Jefferson Davis
in a joint letter in late 1863, "try the souls of men." Addressing
Davis as "Dear Father," they wrote: "Is there no remedy for our
distressed condition? Will not our father, the President, aid and
effectually assist his distressed and sinking children?"

Compassion and treaty obligations required that they be
assisted. And Maxey's other job, Superintendent of Indian Affairs
for the territory, required that he do it. It did not matter to the

Indians that this was a logistical problem virtually beyond Confederate capacities. It only mattered that in this winter, harsher than any they had ever known, they were homeless and suffering, that their husbands, fathers, sons, and brothers were fighting for the Confederacy and that the government had pledged to protect and care for them.

General William Steele, Maxey's predecessor, had begun to cope with the problem even before Maxey arrived. Now as the stream of refugees had turned to a flood, Maxey created an extralegal organization—a unit of his own officers—to deal with the problem, even though there was no law authorizing such an arrangement, and no budget for it. With this extralegal set-up and a bonded agent to receive and disburse funds, he managed to save large numbers of destitute Indians from starvation that winter.

Maxey dreaded the consequences of not feeding them far more than he dreaded the logistical headache of feeding them. "Not only are we by sacred obligations of treaty bound to protect these people," he wrote Henry McCulloch in Texas, "but the dictates of imperative policy demand it. God forbid that the day should come when the Indians turn against us. Alas for Northern Texas. The fairest country the sun ever shone on would be made desolate."

Being a Federal or a Confederate Indian didn't seem to make much difference in this war; there was plenty of suffering to go around. Being a refugee became a common Indian condition North and South. Being neutral didn't make any difference either. Neither pro-Union nor neutral Indians had been tolerated in pro-Confederate Indian Territory in the early days, but had been driven relentlessly from their homes into Kansas. For two stark bitter winters some six thousand of these banished neutral and pro-Union Indians had huddled in Kansas underfed, overexposed, and dying off. When they began coming back with the Union invasion in 1863, it was not with a lot of good will, charity, and forgiveness in their hearts.

4

SHIVERED LIKE A CRUSHED VASE

By mid-March 1864, Maxey was deeply mired in his problems and missing Marilda.

Most of all he was missing Marilda. He was urging her to come up from Paris to be with him in this winter of his discontent, offering to send an escort to meet her on the way. "I have a nice snow for you," he said invitingly.

Bitter winter was still whiplashing the Indian Territory. And there was more in the air than just nasty weather. The Yankees were making big plans to overwhelm Arkansas, Texas, and Louisiana—in effect, to occupy Kirby-Smithdom. Union Major General Nathaniel Banks was planning to drive up the Red River from the south while Major General Frederick Steele was pushing down from the north, the two armies converging on Shreveport, the Confederate headquarters of the Trans-Mississippi West.

Smith, of course, intended to resist this pincer movement

Nathaniel P. Banks: born Massachusetts 1816; received little formal education; admitted to the bar in 1829; entered Massachusetts legislature, rising to speaker of the house; presided over the state's 1853 Constitutional Convention and was elected to the U.S. House of Representatives that same year; speaker of the House 1856; elected governor of Massachusetts in 1858, serving until 1861; at the outbreak of the Civil War, he offered his services to the Union and was appointed major general U.S. Volunteers by President Abraham Lincoln; headed the Department of Annapolis before assuming command of the Department of the Shenandoah; prevented from reinforcing General G.B. McClellan on the Peninsula by the aggressive actions of General T.J. Jackson's Confederates in the Shenandoah Valley; defeated Jackson at Kernstown, Virginia, in March 1862, but fared poorly in subsequent actions; assigned to command the Second Corps in General John Pope's newly-formed Army of Virginia; defeated by Jackson at Cedar Mountain during the Second Bull Run Campaign in August 1862; after Pope's army was dismantled, Banks headed briefly the Military District of Washington before assuming command of the Department of the Gulf; conducted a costly operation against Port Hudson, which fell only after Vicksburg's capture left it untenable; directed the marginally successful Bayou Teche Expedition in the fall of 1863; following the failure of his Red River Expedition in 1864, Banks was relieved by General E.R.S. Canby; received thanks of Congress for Port Hudson; mustered out of volunteer service in 1865; returned to Congress where he served six more terms (not consecutively); declining health forced his retirement from Congress in 1890; he died in Massachusetts in 1894. General Banks was among the most active of the higher-ranking  "political" generals. He was consistently placed in command positions that were beyond his abilities; his personal courage, devotion, and tenacity could not overcome his lack of military training.

and began calling up his forces, including all of the help he could get from Sam Maxey. Maxey had problems enough in Indian Territory without going off to Arkansas to fight Yankee invaders. But that was what this war was all about—fighting. There had been virtually no military action in the Indian Territory since he arrived. Shackled to a desk, he hadn't been in a respectable fight for a long time. Indeed, he had not been in many fights at all. He had been a desk soldier through most of the war up to that time.

Frederick Steele: born New York 1819; graduated from the U.S. Military Academy in 1843, thirtieth in his class of thirty-nine that included U.S. Grant; commissioned 2d lieutenant and posted to infantry; after performing routine frontier and garrison duty, he served with distinction in the Mexican War, winning brevets to 1st

lieutenant and captain and promotion to 1st lieutenant; captain 1855; major 11th Infantry 1861; in the opening stages of the Civil War, he commanded U.S. regulars at the Battle of Wilson's Creek, Missouri; moving to the volunteer organization, he was named colonel of the 8th Iowa Infantry in September 1861; brigadier general U.S. Volunteers January 1862; commanded the District of Southeast Missouri; led a division in the capture of Helena, Arkansas, and in General W.T. Sherman's repulse at Chickasaw Bluffs; major general U.S. Volunteers March 1863; commanded a division in the Army of the Tennessee during the Vicksburg Campaign of 1863; placed in command of the Department of Arkansas; directed the Arkansas portion of the Red River Campaign in the spring of 1864, and after taking Camden was driven back to Little Rock with heavy losses; in 1865 he led a division in General E.R.S. Canby's campaign against Mobile; brevetted through major general U.S. Army, he was finally mustered out of volunteer service in 1867; continued in the regular army as colonel of the 20th Infantry. In 1868, while on leave in California, General Steele suffered an attack of apoplexy and fell from a carriage. He died shortly thereafter.

Maxey pulled together those Indians who were willing to go—the treaties with the Confederate government made their participation in any campaigns outside Indian Territory purely

Sterling Price: born Virginia 1809; attended Hampden-Sydney College and studied law; moved with his family to Missouri in 1830; served in the state legislature and in 1844 was elected to the U.S. House of Representatives; resigned from Congress to lead a regiment of Missouri troops in the Mexican War; promoted to brigadier general of volunteers in 1848; governor of Missouri from 1853 to 1857; he was president of the Missouri convention that voted against secession, but a dispute with radicals prompted his break from the Unionist ranks; offered his services to secessionist Governor C.F. Jackson and accepted command of the Missouri state militia; worked to maintain peace in Missouri, but after negotiations with Union leaders broke down in June 1861, he prepared his troops to oppose Federal forces; combined with General Ben McCulloch's Confederate troops to defeat the Federals at Wilson's Creek, Missouri, in August 1861; captured Lexington, Missouri, in September before retreating into Arkansas; led Missouri troops in General Earl Van Dorn's Confederate force at Elkhorn Tavern, Arkansas, in March 1862; following that defeat, the Missouri troops were mustered into Confederate service and Price was commissioned major general; transferred to Mississippi despite his fervent protest; suffered defeats at Iuka and Corinth before returning to Arkansas; defeated at Helena in 1863; supported General E. Kirby Smith in repulsing General Frederick Steele's Arkansas portion of the Red River Campaign in the spring of 1864; that fall he  led an ambitious cavalry raid into Missouri, but after initial success, was turned back in eastern Kansas; retreating through Indian Territory and northern Texas, Price's remnant returned to Arkansas in December; at the close of the war Price refused to surrender and escaped to Mexico; upon the collapse of Maximilian's empire in 1866, Price returned to Missouri, where he died the following year. Called "Old Pap" by his men, Price was a devoted soldier. While his 1864 raid and subsequent exodus to Mexico have been highly romanticized, his overall military performance was largely unimpressive.

voluntary—and headed for Arkansas. "We are likely to have stirring times," he wrote Henry McCulloch as he left. "The Red River Valley is the prize."

The army that Maxey led into Arkansas was a pick-up force—part of Colonel Richard Gano's brigade of white troops, some Texans loaned by General McCulloch, and Tandy Walker's Choctaw brigade, which had volunteered to go along. Maxey arrived at Prairie D'Ane in south-central Arkansas on April 12. There he found Major General Sterling Price, whom he had been ordered to support, involved with General Steele's Federal troops in what was largely an artillery duel.

As Gano prepared to charge a Union force, Maxey studied the terrain carefully. "Gano," he said finally, "I don't believe that you can take that point."

Gano, being about as manageable as the Indians, charged anyhow, and took the point. Maxey smiled and said, "But it was just because I told him that I didn't think he could take it that he did."

A day or two later Gano was studying the strong Federal force in his front, when Maxey, this time, took it in mind to gallop up the hill in that direction. "General," Gano cautioned him, "don't go up there; you'll be shot to pieces."

But Maxey could be as unmanageable as both Gano and the Indians. "Oh, no, I guess not," he told Gano, and rode away toward the Union position. He was hardly over the brow of the hill when Gano heard the sharp clatter of musketry, and saw Maxey returning at full gallop. As he pounded past, Maxey called out, "Gano I guess you are right." The desk general was getting his taste of battle and learning some things.

Maxey's assignment at Prairie D'Ane was to help check the Federal advance on Camden by pecking away at Steele's rear, while avoiding a general engagement. Price didn't wish him to risk a major set-to with the Union army, not just yet anyhow.

Near Poison Springs on April 18, Maxey found a fight that

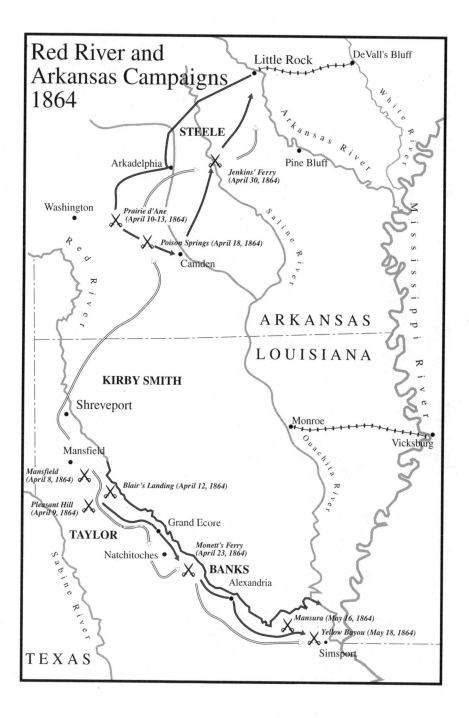

Red River and
Arkansas Campaigns
1864

DeVall's Bluff

Little Rock

White River

STEELE

Arkadelphia

Arkansas River

Pine Bluff

*Jenkins' Ferry
(April 30, 1864)*

Washington

*Prairie d'Ane
(April 10-13, 1864)*

Saline River

Poison Springs (April 18, 1864)

Red River

Camden

ARKANSAS

LOUISIANA

Mississippi River

KIRBY SMITH

Shreveport

Monroe

Vicksburg

Ouachita River

Mansfield

*Mansfield
(April 8, 1864)*

Blair's Landing (April 12, 1864)

*Pleasant Hill
(April 9, 1864)*

Grand Ecore

TAYLOR

Natchitoches

*Monett's Ferry
(April 23, 1864)*

BANKS

Alexandria

Sabine River

Mansura (May 16, 1864)

Yellow Bayou (May 18, 1864)

Simsport

TEXAS

beautifully met the requirements. Union troops were moving a major wagon train on the old military road about ten miles from Camden. A Confederate force under the command of Brigadier General John Sappington Marmaduke was out on the

John Sappington Marmaduke: born Missouri 1833; attended both Yale and Harvard before entering the U.S. Military Academy, graduating in 1857, thirtieth in his class of thirty-eight; commissioned 2d lieutenant and posted to infantry, he participated in the Mormon Expedition; still on frontier duty at the outbreak of the Civil War, he resigned his commission to become colonel in the Missouri state militia; fought at Boonville in 1861, but resigned his state commission to enter Confederate Service; commissioned 1st lieutenant; named lieutenant colonel of the 1st Arkansas Infantry Battalion; promoted to colonel, 3rd Confederate Infantry; wounded in an outstanding performance at Shiloh in April 1862; transferred to the

Trans-Mississippi, he commanded the cavalry in General T.C. Hindman's Corps, Army of the West; brigadier general November 1862; led a cavalry division that raided twice into Missouri; fought at Helena and Little Rock; he dueled with and killed fellow Confederate General Lucius Walker at Little Rock in September 1863, for which he was arrested but soon released; during the Red River Campaign in the spring of 1864 Marmaduke's cavalry, with General Samuel Bell Maxey's Texans and Indians, opposed General Frederick Steele's Arkansas operations at Poison Springs and Jenkins' Ferry; that fall he commanded a cavalry division in General Sterling Price's Missouri invasion; in November he was captured while directing a rear guard action in Kansas; imprisoned at Fort Warren, Massachusetts, for the remainder of the war, he was nonetheless promoted to major general in March 1865, becoming the last Confederate officer to be elevated to that rank; released from prison in July 1865; he worked in the insurance business after the war and edited an agricultural journal in Missouri; elected governor of that state in 1884; General Marmaduke died in office in 1887. He was a gifted cavalry commander whose efforts largely escaped recognition outside the isolated Trans-Mississippi.

road laying the train under siege. Maxey was ordered to the scene to assume command and finish the job. When he arrived, Marmaduke was preparing to pitch into the train's large escort of Federal artillery, cavalry, and infantry. Maxey's first command on assuming command was an act of intelligence and tact of the sort that had become one of his hallmarks: he ordered Marmaduke to continue seeing to the disposition of troops and running the show, since Marmaduke had started the business and knew the layout far better than he. Maxey would deploy in any way his junior thought wise. Together Marmaduke and Maxey fashioned a little masterpiece. Not a false step was made, not a position was attacked that was not taken. The road was gained, the enemy was routed, and the entire train of more than two hundred wagons and a battery of six field pieces was abandoned and seized, forcing Steele to retire. The haul was a cornucopia; the train was "laden with corn, bacon, stolen bed-quilts, women's and children's clothing, hogs, geese, and all the et ceteras of unscrupulous plunder," said one of Gano's officers. "A perfect success," agreed General Price, a "brilliant affair."

Colonel Tandy Walker, commanding the Choctaw Brigade, pointed with particular pride to Private Dickson Wallace, who in the pursuit mounted a gun and gave the first war whoop of the fight. It was followed, Walker was proud to report, by a succession of whoops "as made the woods reverberate for miles around."

Maxcy returned to Fort Towson, cranked up his printing press and gave a few joyous whoops of his own. He believed that the Choctaw brigade fighting on the Confederate left had "nobly, gallantly, gloriously" done its duty, and he was going to tell everybody so. He called the campaign "more stupendous in proportions than any ever heretofore inaugurated by the enemy in the Trans-Mississippi Department.... The design was no less than to hold, occupy, and possess the whole of the Red

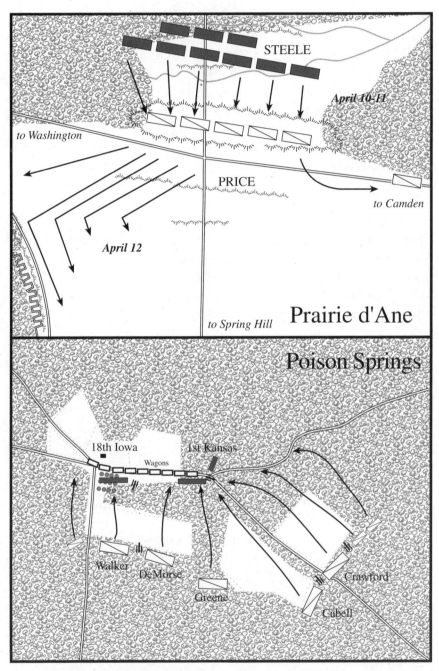

This map was based primarily on written records. Anyone with more information on these areas, please inform the publisher.

River Valley, with its untold resources. An immense column moved through Louisiana, another through Arkansas. Everywhere the enemy was met, and everywhere our arms were victorious. The campaign has been shivered like a crushed vase.... Your action has been glorious. You have made yourselves a name in history."

Having said all this, Maxey resigned.

He had been reading the promotion orders, and he didn't like what he saw—or rather, didn't see: his name was not there.

Maxey's sensitivity was broad enough to resent slights, and he felt slighted. "Now I find Brigadiers junior to me promoted for conduct in the Arkansas campaign," he complained to Smith in his letter of resignation. He was offended. His friends at home in north Texas were reading the promotions list, too, and writing to ask why he was not on it, and he couldn't tell them. Was this his reward? For all the troubles heaped on him, some of them so great that he hadn't thought it proper even to mention them to headquarters?

Maxey's letter of resignation triggered a chain reaction. Many officers in his command, when they heard of it, were more upset by the prospect of his leaving than he was by being passed over. They began signing and circulating petitions urging that he not be permitted to resign.

In Maxey, the petitioners insisted, were united the qualifications and requirements necessary for the job as far as they could be expected to be found in any one person. They said he enjoyed the entire confidence of the Indian nations and of the army, which he had so successfully commanded. A petition from one battalion bore some nineteen names, with this explanation: "All the members of the 1st Battalion express the greatest willingness to sign the above petition if space would permit. There are 200 present."

The ever-ambitious Douglas Cooper was more upset by these developments than anybody—but for an entirely different reason. Wanting Maxey's job, he resented the petitions. So he confiscated them and sent them to Maxey, charging that they were contrary to regulations, calculated to compromise Maxey, injure himself, and sow dissension in the command detrimental to the service.

In a letter to Smith, Cooper explained that he returned the mischievous petitions "not because I desired to throw any obstacle in the way of Gen Maxey's promotion, which I should be glad to see, but because I considered it in violation of...Army Regulations." He argued that the petitions heaped extraordinary praise on Maxey and reflected unfavorably on his predecessors or anyone else "hitherto found willing to undertake the arduous duties of Commandant of the Dist Ind Terry," which he hoped would soon include himself. He claimed to be doing Maxey a favor.

Maxey knew nothing of the petitions until they arrived in the mail from Cooper. However, he must have been gratified to see them and not at all surprised that Cooper had confiscated them.

Major George Williamson, Smith's assistant adjutant general and a good friend of Maxey's, was at headquarters in Shreveport opening the morning mail when Maxey's letter of resignation arrived. When he read it, he started violently. It was all a terrible mistake. Immediately he wrote Maxey a confidential letter. Trusting that their friendship and past service together would justify it, Williamson told him he had pulled the letter of resignation so Smith wouldn't see it. He explained that Maxey's promotion had long been in the works, and he thought it in Maxey's best interest not to let the resignation come to Smith's attention. The petitions, of course, were not yet circulating.

In truth, Smith had ordered Maxey's promotion weeks before, effective the day of the battle of Poison Springs, making him senior to every other major general appointed since then. But Maxey had been victimized by the red tape-ism he said had never much bothered him.

Smith had no reason to be anything but satisfied with Maxey. As early as January 25, he had written him, through Williamson, that "since you assumed command there appears to be an improvement of affairs in the Indian Territory." On June 8, he wrote him personally to apologize for the promotion mixup. "I regretted very much that your appointment as major general, was not more promptly forwarded to you," he said. It had been delayed through an oversight in the office. "Let me express to you my satisfaction and thanks," he wrote, "for the manner in which you have administered your District. I know the annoyances and difficulties with which you have been environed. I feel that a great improvement has already been made. There probably remains much yet to be accomplished. You may rely upon every assistance in my power to support you in your reforms." Maxey, now a new major general with new seniority, withdrew his resignation.

5

DOING WHAT INDIANS DO BEST

That was settled, then. But the problems had by no means gone away. Cooper was still trying to replace him, there was a summer's campaign to tend to, there were still not enough guns and too many destitute Indians to feed. None of that had changed. Maxey wrote Marilda not ten days after the letter of praise and promotion from Smith, telling her of "a baker's dozen of troubles" he had endured that day. He had quelled a mixed crowd of drunken Indians and whites, his horse had been sick, he had taken the wrong road on the prairie in the dark, stalled in a mud hole, broken both single trees (vital parts of his wagon harness), and hadn't sat down to supper until eleven o'clock that night. The only bright spot in the day had been Stand Watie's promotion to brigadier general, effective May 6, on Maxey's recommendation.

Maxey was full of plans for a major offensive against the Yankees that summer, big plans—no less than clearing them out of Indian Territory and reclaiming Forts Smith and Gibson. Union control of those two strategic forts on the Arkansas River stuck in Maxey's craw. He believed they should never have been lost in the first place, and that they could and ought to be won back. He had wanted to do it on the momentum of the victory at Poison Springs in April, but Smith had vetoed it. Maxey believed that the Union garrisons in both strongholds were weak, and that they could be retaken. It had been his goal from the start to reorganize and strengthen his army, wrest back the forts, and drive the Yankees from the territory.

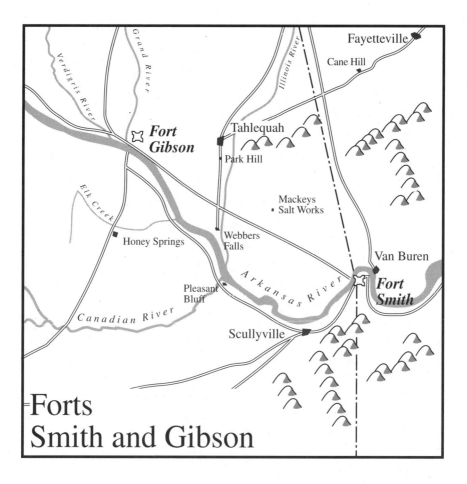

Forts Smith and Gibson

But by summer reality had set in, and Maxey's goals had to be scaled back. The Union army's Red River campaign to seize Louisiana and Texas had failed, but a major Confederate offensive to retake the forts seemed out of the question. The best Maxey could hope for by mid-summer was to hold Union troops in check at the two forts and, with luck, force an evacuation.

Maxey simply didn't have the resources to match his ambitions, and he was never going to have them. The guns had never come. He didn't have the means to mount a major campaign of any kind. He couldn't even keep his command in clothes. He must settle for letting the Indians do what they did best—harass the enemy from below the Arkansas River, hitting and running and hoping for a Federal blunder that would give them an opening to recoup some of the losses of 1863. That's what the war in the Indian Territory had come down to by 1864—hit-and-run raids—and Maxey knew it.

It was regrettable. The Indians finally had in Maxey an aggressive commander with drive and skill—a West Pointer who knew what he was about—and the best they could manage was a guerrilla war. So be it, they would wage a guerrilla war. Fortunately Maxey had in Watie one of the best guerrilla fighters in the business.

If he couldn't retake Forts Smith and Gibson, Maxey felt he could at least worry the Yankee garrisons to death, seal them up inside, deny them vital resources, attack their supply wagons, burn their hay, cut their telegraph lines, ambush patrols, intercept mail and supplies, intimidate pro-Union civilians in the area, and make life generally miserable.

To this end, he kept abreast of what was going on inside Forts Smith and Gibson by reading the *Era*, a Union newspaper. "I have as little use for the *Era* and as little faith in Yankee papers generally as any man in the Confederacy," he explained. But he found it expedient to credit some of the news he found there, particularly about the arrivals and departures of supply boats.

As Maxey at Fort Towson kept track of the comings and goings, he sent Cooper and Watie with their Indian troops, and Gano with his white soldiers, out to meet the boats before they docked. Gano attacked a Union detachment about five miles from Fort Smith on July 27, and routed it.

"In brilliancy and dash and completeness of success," Maxey exulted, skittering on the sticky edge of hyperbole, "[the action] has not been surpassed in this year of brilliant victories." He said he did not believe that the enemy would throw out anything stronger than a reconnaissance in force after this.

As Gano was raiding, Cooper was demonstrating in front of Fort Smith to divert attention from Watie, who was out back interfering with Federal hay-cutting and stock-pasturing activities.

Disrupting Yankee hay harvests was all right, but it was nothing compared with the opportunity Watie saw paddle-wheeling up the Arkansas River on June 15. It was a beauty, a Federal stern-wheeler slapping upriver from Little Rock and groaning with supplies for Fort Gibson. This was the sort of thing that the Confederacy's new and only Indian brigadier lived for. He would curl his bow legs around the sides of a pony any day for a prize like that.

Watie was waiting to claim the prize as it thrashed around the bend of the river near Pleasant Bluff, about five miles below the juncture with the Canadian River. Its trip had been an ill-kept secret. Maxey may even have read about it in the *Era*. And Watie had set up well ahead of time on the high steep bluffs overlooking a broad curve in the river below. He carefully concealed his three guns in the brush on the heights about a hundred yards apart and commanding the river from bank to bank. The Yankees would never know what hit them.

The steamboat, the *J.R. Williams*, was overloaded and underprotected, just the sort of condition Watie appreciated. It was ordinarily a troop ferry, but on this trip it was laden with commissary and quartermaster goods valued at about $120,000. There were thousands of yards of cloth and linen aboard, many pounds of cotton yarn, blankets, shawls, skirts, harnesses, boots, a thousand barrels of flour, fifteen tons of bacon shoulders, and a large assortment of tinware. Escorting it was a small force of only one officer and twenty-five infantrymen, with no cavalry to reconnoiter the shore. It was a sitting duck.

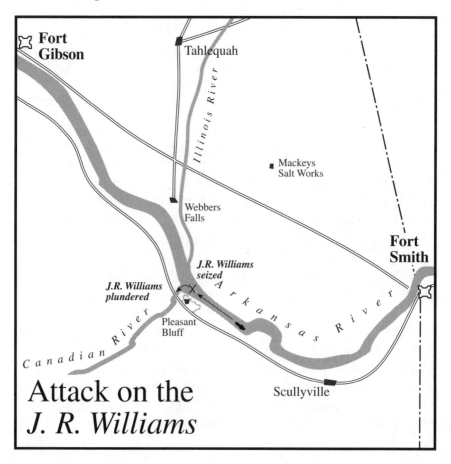

Attack on the
J. R. Williams

The river curved to the south side of its wide meander belt at Pleasant Bluff. That would bring the stern-wheeler in close to the southern shore right under Watie's waiting guns. As it rounded into the curve, the guns opened up. The first salvos rocked the boat, raked the pilot house, smashed into the smoke stack, and disabled the boiler. A cascading geyser of steam erupted, flooding the decks. The boat appeared about to sink or explode. The pilot frantically ran the stricken vessel aground on the north bank opposite the Confederate ambush, and the infantry escort hit the shore and took cover in the woods. With no chance of saving the boat, they started for Fort Smith.

After the Indians off-loaded the plunder and burned the boat, Watie's troubles began. He had absolutely no control from that point on over his cantankerous soldiers, particularly the Creeks and Seminoles. They gleefully rifled the loot and began making off with it. About sixty of Watie's own Cherokees were particularly taken with the tinware. Every one of their horses virtually disappeared under a layer of washtubs, stew kettles, coffeepots, washpans, tin plates, cups, and dippers—items in much demand and short supply in Indian Territory.

By this time Federal troops were out on the road headed for the scene. As the Cherokees with the tinware were rattle-banging across a two mile wide strip of open prairie bounded on either side by thick timber, a strong force of Union cavalry burst out of the woods behind and charged. The Cherokees lit out for the woods ahead in a deafening clatter, throwing off pots and pans as they went to lighten the load and enhance celerity. It was pandemonium, one of the noisiest retreats of the war.

Watie had ordered up wagons from General Cooper to haul away what plunder was left. But late in the day when it appeared that Federal troops might arrive first, he set fire to the goods and prepared to abandon them and flee. As he was leaving, he ordered George Washington Grayson, the young Creek captain, to organize a suitable number of Creeks to remain on watch at the site until sundown—to warn the retreating force of any impending attack.

Grayson would one day be chief of the Creek Nation. But on this day in June 1864, he was barely twenty-one, the youngest captain in the Indian service. He was willing to do as ordered, but he was bucking that strong-willed Indian resistance to anything resembling discipline. There was frantic activity in every direction, every man in hot haste to be part of the getaway.

Stay here with you, kid? was the sentiment that greeted Grayson's pleas for volunteers. Not on your life, sonny. Grayson knew beforehand that he probably hadn't a ghost of a chance of persuading anybody to stay with him, but he made the effort anyhow. When everybody had cleared out, the site was left to approaching darkness and Grayson—a detachment of one, all chief and no Indians.

The sun couldn't set fast enough for Grayson. He found himself "the none-too-willing 'monarch of all I surveyed,'" sitting alone and lonely "in the almost oppressive silence of the on-coming but to me, too pokey sunset." He looked and looked, but saw neither an enemy, nor a sun going down. The "awe-inspiring silence" that prevailed "in depressing supremacy all around," particularly grieved him. The only sound was the chirp of a solitary cricket. Then "at last! at last! the wished for moment came. The sun after reddening for a few minutes, sank behind the western horizon...."

An instant later Grayson was out of there.

6

THE MILLION-DOLLAR
WAGON RAID

Richard Gano had a somewhat similar problem. For some time he had wanted out of there too, out of Indian Territory altogether. It was sorry duty, made worse by a bitter running dispute he had been having with his subordinate, Charles DeMorse, who felt he ought to be in command of the territory's white brigade instead of Gano.

Gano would have been long gone already had it not been for Sam Maxey. Gano had asked for a transfer out of the district only a month before. He had told Maxey he was dissatisfied with service in the district, tired of the inefficiency and the grumbling.

He had said that he would "sacrifice all I have and am in this life, and life itself before I would be subjugated by the Yankees." But he did not believe that was reason enough to remain in Indian Territory, where the greatest privations and least credit existed and where his white soldiers lacked confidence in the Indian troops. Gano believed that earlier in the summer, if he had had the forage and water for his horses, he could have taken Fort Smith. He was disgusted it hadn't happened. "We had them so badly scared," he believed, "that they would have crossed the river & evacuated the place,

Richard Gano: born Kentucky 1830; attended Bacon College in Kentucky, Bethany College in Virginia, and Louisville University Medical School; practiced medicine in Kentucky before removing to Texas in 1859, where he raised cattle and fought Indians; elected to the state legislature in 1860; at the outbreak of the Civil War he raised two companies of cavalry for Confederate service; Gano's squadron joined John Hunt Morgan's command in the 1862 Kentucky invasion and in the

Tullahoma Campaign; colonel, 7th Kentucky Cavalry, 1863; ill, he returned to Texas; given command of Texas state cavalry operating in the Indian Territory; participated with distinction under General Samuel Bell Maxey in the Camden Campaign, in which he was wounded, 1864; returning to the Indian Territory he fought near Fort Smith, and at Fort Gibson and Cabin Creek; during the latter, one of the most successful cavalry raids of the war, he was senior officer but prudently deferred command to cooperate with the Indian troops led by General Stand Watie; originally promoted to brigadier general by order of General E. Kirby Smith, commander of the Trans-Mississippi, Gano received his official appointment in March 1865; after the war he resided briefly in Kentucky before returning to Texas; active in the United Confederate Veterans, General Gano became a minister in the Christian Church in 1868, serving as such until his death at Dallas in 1913. Both Morgan and Maxey praised Gano's ability and execution of duty. Despite problems of poor equipage and frequent desertion, Gano maintained a high level of fighting effectiveness in his command of Texas state troops.

before they would have ventured out to fight us."

Maxey liked Gano and would hate to lose him. They had much in common. Both were Kentuckians by birth. Gano was raised on a farm in the bluegrass state, where he had gone on to get his medical degree. Like Maxey, he had migrated to Texas in the late 1850s, and like Maxey he had been elected to the Texas legislature. Also like Maxey, he had been granted authority to raise troops when the war came. While Gano was a devout Christian and had leanings toward the ministry, he didn't let the Ten Commandments interfere with his fighting. Maxey liked all of that about Gano.

"I am aware that there are very many things to render service here unpleasant," Maxey had written him, "that there are but few comforts or resources to be got here—it is a Side District." Gano might not win the "brilliant evanescent reputation" he might elsewhere, Maxey agreed, but "you will in standing here between the Enemy and your own people as a wall acquire character that will last you through life."

Gano liked Maxey too and had stayed, and now, in September 1864, he was feeling a little better about things because there was the prospect of a fight. Maxey had just ordered Gano and Watie north to raise some hell with the Yankees, something Gano had long been lobbying for.

"It is true," he had written Maxey in late August, "that many of my men are dismounted, barefooted & unarmed, but they would be better satisfied if actively employed, than idling in camps. And there would be a pretty fair chance to capture arms, horses & clothing"—maybe even shoes. "We ought to be up there now," he had argued. "The river is fordable and we are burning away the light of day, or the working season. Say to us go and success attend you." Maxey finally said go in the middle of September.

Gano and Watie had learned that a mammoth Yankee wagon train was moving out of Fort Scott in Kansas bound for

A Union wagon train.

Fort Gibson. It was a whopper, three hundred wagons loaded with as much as a million and a half dollars in clothing, boots, shoes, arms, ammunition, blankets, foodstuffs, liquor, and medicine. It had left Fort Scott on September 12, under the command of Major Henry Hopkins, with an escort of 260 Kansas cavalry.

It was a target that cried to be attacked, and Gano and Watie met on the thirteenth to consider what could be done to oblige it. They agreed that each would command his own troops, but act together and in harmony. The next morning they set out to meet the slow-moving wagon train, Gano at the head of twelve hundred white troops, and Watie leading eight hundred Indians.

Major Hopkins was not sanguine about any of this. He was sure of an enemy attack at some point along the way. He heard that a Confederate force was on the march, but he didn't know how strong it was or where it was. He called for all of the troop support he could get, and at Baxter Springs one hundred Federal Cherokees joined the escort.

The Confederate force reached Prairie Springs the night of September 14, and the banks of the Arkansas about noon on the fifteenth. The river was so swollen it took them six hours of hard work to cross. On the sixteenth they forded the Verdigris, attacked a Federal hay camp, and engaged in a brief running fight with Federal cavalry.

But where was the wagon train? It was overdue. Had they missed it? On the eighteenth, Gano rode out with a detachment of four hundred men and two guns to try to find it, while the Indian brigade under Watie began preparing for battle, "making medicine," painting their faces, and waiting for Greenbrier Joe, their chief shaman, to affirm that the omens were propitious.

Gano found the Federal wagon train camped at Cabin Creek some fifty miles from Fort Gibson. He sent a courier back for

Watie to bring up the rest of the force and the other four guns, and Watie arrived about midnight. Hopkins had arrived at Cabin Creek with an escort that had swelled to over six hundred whites and Indians. But he still had no idea how large a Confederate force was out there in the night.

It was a glorious cloudless moonlit night, the battlefield bathed by a God-given skylight. When the Confederates opened fire about one o'clock in the morning on September 19, Hopkins learned for the first time that the enemy was not only out there, but with artillery—a depressing fact.

The first rebel charge stampeded the Union teamsters, who began cutting single mules from the teams and riding them away at a gallop back toward Fort Scott. That made it impossible for Hopkins to move the abandoned wagons. When after daybreak the Confederates took possession of the road in the train's rear, it was all over.

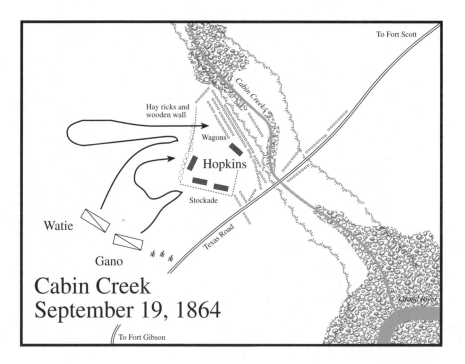

To Fort Scott

Cabin Creek

Hay ricks and wooden wall

Wagons

Hopkins

Stockade

Watie

Gano

Texas Road

Grand River

**Cabin Creek
September 19, 1864**

To Fort Gibson

Gano and Watie now had to work fast. With 130 wagons that had been captured and were able to roll, they started back toward the Arkansas River. As they hurried away with the stolen train, they ran an empty wagon over a rocky place for two hours to create the illusion that they were parking for the night. By the time they successfully crossed the river, two weeks from the day they had left, Gano reckoned they had marched over four hundred miles, killed ninety-seven Yankees, captured over a hundred prisoners, burned six thousand tons of hay and assorted reapers and mowers, and brought back all those loaded wagons and 740 mules. He counted the cost at six of his men killed and forty-five wounded, three of them mortally.

Elias Boudinot, the Cherokee delegate to the Confederate Congress in Richmond, wrote Watie that the "whole country is alive with the glorious news of your success." With a smile of satisfaction, Watie said he believed this blow "will be severely felt by the enemy"—an outcome a guerilla warrior covets.

Young Captain Grayson had so loudly cheered his men on in the smoke of battle that he could later speak only in a hoarse whisper. His body also ached. He had spent endless days in the saddle coming and going and then fighting. When it was over he said it had been "certainly the most trying expedition I have ever been engaged in." But it had all been worth it.

At Fort Towson Maxey worked his printing press overtime cranking out praise. "For gallantry, energy, enterprise, dash, and judgment, and completeness of success this raid has not been surpassed during the war," he exulted. He rejoiced in particular that it had been such a magnificent show of "perfect harmony and good will" between the white and Indian troops, "all striving for the common good of our beloved country." Maxey couldn't say enough about the leadership of "the gallant and chivalrous Gano" and "the noble old hero, Stand Watie."

As a morale booster, it was hard to beat. Coming with

Watie's capture of the *J.R. Williams* in June, it created a wave of euphoria followed by wholesale Indian reenlistments. The plunder alone had been worth the trip to Cabin Creek. It included two hundred Sharps rifles and four hundred pistols—Maxey would get his guns wherever he could find them. From the 130 wagons brought back over the Arkansas, Gano and Watie re-clothed their tattered brigades. Maxey saw this as "a perfect god send, as the command was literally ragged." When news of the raid reached Mrs. Watie in Texas, she wrote her husband: "I thought I would send some clothes, but I hear you have done better."

The Indian troops had never been very presentable. They tended to look "more like Siberian exiles than soldiers." When they caught a prisoner, explained Grayson, they generally stripped him clean, as he was invariably better dressed than they, and decked him instead in "such of our own duds as he could wear." Maxey's command had been so threadbare before the million-dollar wagon raid that he had published appeals for clothing in the *Dallas Herald*.

So the summer ended. It had not been a summer of the kind of warfare West Point had taught Maxey to wage, or that he would have preferred. It had been but a series of Indian raids, the best to be hoped for under the circumstances. But Maxey could summarize the summer with some pride: A steamboat packed with valuable Federal stores had been captured and destroyed; important Federal mail had been intercepted; an entire Federal regiment had been virtually demolished in sight of the guns of Fort Smith; many prisoners, horses, mules, cattle, guns, and wagons had been appropriated here and there; countless ricks of hay had been torched; and the summer had ended with that magnificent million-dollar wagon raid. He hadn't retaken the two forts, but he had kept the Yankees locked up inside. He was satisfied.

As his worn and tattered forces raided through the country,

Maxey had been desk bound, "heels over head in business" as he put it—office work. "I have been on the tread mill of labor all my life," he wrote Marilda, "and I suppose I will have to stay to the end."

In late August, between the two big raids of the summer, he had written a long report on the status of the Indian Territory for S.S. Scott, the Confederate Commissioner of Indian Affairs in Richmond. Scott was impressed, and told Smith so. "I regard the Indian Country as being in much better condition now and the Indians more hopeful and nearer contented than they have been for the last two years," Scott wrote Smith.

It was a gratifying state of affairs, and Scott attributed it in large part "to the wise and judicious course" charted by Maxey. "From his report which has just been submitted to me," Scott wrote, "it seems that he well understands Indian character."

7

THE DAMNED NUISANCE

There was a deeply disturbing counterpoint to the summer of success in the field and the praise from the commissioner. Rumors were flying that Maxey's days were surely numbered this time. It was the Douglas Cooper factor again. "They are giving Gen'l Maxey fits," an officer in the Choctaw brigade wrote in late August. "I will do all I can for him for I consider he has more generalship about him in one day than Cooper would have in twelve months."

Maxey held his counsel as long as he could in the face of the rumors, but by the end of October he figured he had to know what was going on. So he wrote Brigadier General William R. Boggs, Smith's chief of staff, a private letter.

Rumors, he told Boggs, "have been rife in a quiet sort of way for the last two weeks that Gen'l Cooper was to supersede me." He said this had been causing no little excitement there and in north Texas, and that he had been telling people he had no knowledge of any change.

"Having succeeded in perfecting a system approaching order, which has been wrought out of chaos," he wrote Boggs, "it would be a great injustice to me now at the harvest, to deprive me of the fruits of my labor, and that by a summary order thrusting me aside, virtually saying that I had failed as a District Commander." If there was a prominent or intelligent man conversant with the facts who was not gratified by his success with the command, Maxey hadn't heard of him. "God knows," he told Boggs, "it has only been a command of incessant labor and vexation...and it has been to every man who has commanded here." He said that since the rumors paralyzed his administration to a certain extent, what, in effect, do they amount to? He would be glad to know the facts.

The facts were that the rumors were true. Since early August, Smith had been sitting on those explicit orders from Richmond to replace Maxey with Cooper. Since the idea was as repugnant to Smith as it was to Maxey, he simply hadn't implemented them. Finally in early October he wrote Richmond asking that they be revoked.

"I believe that serious injury would result to the service were this order enforced," he said frankly. "I have delayed its publication awaiting further instructions." Smith praised Maxey's handling of the district, citing his skill, his judgment, and his successes: "I have satisfactory evidence for believing that he gives satisfaction to both Indian and white troops. His removal, besides being an injustice to him, would be a misfortune to the department." Richmond's response was a summary no: The order "is deemed imperative and must be carried into effect."

So Smith continued to sit on it. Maxey, with his job hanging by a thread, prepared to attend another meeting of the Grand Council at the Armstrong Academy. He would go from there to Fort Washita, Boggy Depot, and visit Gano's brigade on the way back. He would get out of the office, tour the district. At Armstrong Academy, on Saturday, November 5, he read to the Indians the report he had written for Scott and reviewed the past year in detail in a three-hour address. The Indian leaders listened attentively and afterward said they would vote on his administration on the following Monday.

The weather had been miserable the first two days of Maxey's trip, and the third day was cold and raw. But it had then turned beautiful; maybe that was a good omen. Maxey left for Fort Washita with hopes that it would prove so. At Washita he was greeted with a major general's salute of eight guns, and remained there three days before moving on to Boggy Depot and then to Gano's brigade. Maxey wrote Marilda enroute, and closed, as he often did, with a kiss for their little adopted daughter, Dora: "Tell her I saw a heap of 'big Indians' with paint in their hair."

After Maxey left, the Indians with the paint in their hair met again and fully endorsed his administration, civil and military. Maxey was gratified. "My course," he wrote Smith, "has been indorsed by the department commander, the Commissioner of Indian Affairs, the council of the tribes and nations in alliance, the people in the contiguous portions of Texas and Arkansas, and above all, by my own conscience, and whatever action the War Department or the President may see fit to take, I shall now rest satisfied."

It was well he felt that way, because Smith could not sit on the direct order to turn the Territory over to Cooper much longer. He held off as long as he could, until February 1865, when an agitated and disgusted Cooper went to Richmond in person to see his friend Davis. Soon after, Davis ordered Smith to issue the orders immediately. Smith had successfully stalled for half a year.

In orders issued on February 14, Stand Watie was directed to assume command of the Indian division and Cooper was elevated into Maxey's job. Smith said nothing in praise of Cooper, but told the war department in Richmond that he "enters upon this duty when affairs in that district are in a better condition than have before existed since my arrival in this department. This favorable change is due in a great measure to the successful administration of General Maxey." Smith pledged his support to Cooper, but said, "the change has not the concurrence of my judgment, and I believe will not result beneficially." Cooper was entering on the post he had coveted for so long to a cold and vacant welcome.

From the time the rumors started in October that Cooper was to replace Maxey, letters of support and regret, even of horror, began flowing in to Maxey. When it appeared inevitable, in early 1865, Maxey was deluged with letters. If Cooper was popular with the Chickasaws and the Choctaws, his popularity extended to few, if any, of the white officers in the command. Many of them wanted out. They preferred Maxey; he had treated them well, and they disliked and feared Cooper.

A battalion commander wrote Maxey in October, "we are willing to go anywhere to serve any way in any capacity rather than stay here.... Any place short of Pandemonium will suit us better if you are gone.... If you go for Gods sake take us. I know Gen. C_____'s feelings so well if you are gone he will make your friends left behind feel the might of his power." The letter scored Cooper's disposition "to rule or ruin. I do not want to serve under him if I can help myself."

"It is with a feeling of regret to part with one who has ever been so kind as yourself and who has so considerately looked over my many faults," another wrote Maxey in January. "I feel that I can nowhere be so pleasantly situated as I have been with you or find a Commanding officer for whom I have the same esteem and respect as for yourself."

The letters kept coming. A surgeon in his command wrote

Maxey to say he wanted to go with him, wherever that might be: "It is my preference to be in your command, having served more pleasantly there, than in that of any other officer under whom I have been placed since the war." The surgeon spoke of Maxey's "courteous and gentlemanly bearing towards me" for the past thirteen months, and of the "unpleasant feeling between Brig. Gen. D.H. Cooper and myself...unpleasant in the extreme," and predating Maxey. If he couldn't go where Maxey went, then anywhere else would be better than remaining in Indian Territory. Captain R.W. Lee, whom Maxey had appointed as his inspector general soon after taking command in the Territory, wrote: "I cannot express the regret I feel at the loss of yourself, as my commander.... I know of no General who can supply your place, or under whom I shall be willing to hold position. I wish I could go with you."

Even Maxey's adjutant, who had been passing all of these letters of appreciation and panic on to his general, wanted out. "Our official and personal relations have been most agreeable," he said in a letter of his own. "Your distinguished ability as a military commander as well as an administrative officer has won for you the respect and admiration of all who know you....your uniform courtesy and kindness." He asked to be relieved if Maxey was, and ordered "to report to you wherever you may go."

Maxey's job was done; he was through in Indian Territory. Smith sent him to take command of a division especially organized for him in Texas, amid signs that the war was winding down and that Cooper had won a pointless victory. Whatever happened didn't matter much anymore. Maxey knew, as he had said at year's end, that "troubles in this Territory will never cease." They were not likely to cease even with the end of the war.

What had it all amounted to? Somehow Maxey had been just the right choice for the Indians. His free and easy style had suited them exactly. Thanks in large part to him, the Confederate Indians remained loyal to the end. Indeed, Watie was the last Confederate general to surrender in the war.

Maxey had posted more hours at a desk than in a saddle, and had won few laurels for himself on the battlefield—only at Poison Springs, his one and only battle the entire time. But he had done and said things the Indians would always remember as courageous and noble. He had looked upon their destitution with genuine compassion and had tried to do something about it.

He had kept them moving, letting them fight their kind of war and supporting them as best he could. There had been no decisive victories anywhere, no Federal army was annihilated or even defeated. He never recaptured Forts Smith and Gibson or forced their evacuation. He hadn't even been able to get the Indians all the guns they needed. But the series of limited raids that he had orchestrated, capitalizing on the Indian talent for hit and run warfare, had neutralized Federal forces in the territory, disrupted their supply lines, and denied them vital resources. It could have been argued that but for him the war might have ended for the Indians a year earlier than it did.

In short, Maxey had managed to make himself a damned nuisance—not a bad record at all for the cadet who had finished next to last in his class at West Point. But he wasn't through. He still had that one final goal he had set for himself following the Mexican War—to go to the United States Senate.

In 1875, he achieved even that. Elected as a Democratic senator from Texas, he went to Washington and six years later was reelected to a second term. One of his main interests in the Senate continued to be Indian affairs. It was a time of turmoil on the frontier, a time of violent uprisings by the Plains Indians—the time of the Custer massacre at the Little Big Horn. Maxey knew more about Indians than most of his Senate colleagues, and he continued to speak on the subject— earnestly, emphatically, and at great length, urging that

Sam Bell Maxey in his senatorial years.

Indians be handled with a hand of iron covered by a glove of silk.

He would not be elected to a third term, but would return to Texas, where he devoted the rest of his years to the law. He became a close student of Texas history, and author of works about the past, which he had helped to shape. He died in 1895, and was buried with honor on a sunny Sunday afternoon in Paris, Texas.

FURTHER READING

Abel, Annie Heloise. *The American Indian as Slaveholder and Secessionist* and *The American Indian as Participant in the Civil War*. Cleveland: Arthur H. Clark Company, 1919. These two volumes, published seventy-five years ago, are still the standard work on the slaveholding Indians and their participation in the Civil War. For a short treatment of the subject by the same author, see "Indians in the Civil War." *American Historical Review* 15 (1910): 281–96.

Anderson, Thomas F. "The Indian Territory 1861 to 1865." *Confederate Veteran* 4 (1896): 85–87. A short review of the Indian Territory during the war, from a Confederate point of view.

Cantrell, Mark Lea (Beau), and Mac Harris, eds. *Kepis and Turkey Calls: An Anthology of the War between the States in Indian Territory*. Oklahoma City: Western Heritage Books, 1982. A collection of articles by various authors on a variety of aspects of the Civil War in Indian Territory, with good connecting and explanatory lead-ins by the editors.

Chronicles of Oklahoma. Various issues. This quarterly published by the Oklahoma Historical Society, has run many excellent articles over the years by leading scholars about the Civil War in Indian Territory. Taken together they represent a reliable, exhaustive source. Some of the most useful of these articles, listed alphabetically by author, include:

> Anderson, Mabel Washburne. "General Stand Watie." Vol. 10 (1932). Anderson also authored a biography, *Life of Stand Watie*, published in 1915. A new, first-rate modern biography is much needed.

> Ashcraft, Allan C. "Confederate Indian Department Conditions in August, 1964." Vol. 41 (1963): 270–85.

> _____. "Confederate Indian Troop Conditions in 1864." Vol. 41 (1963–64): 442–49. This and the preceding citation give a good combined picture of conditions in Maxey's command in the last year of the war.

> Banks, Dean. "Civil War Refugees from Indian Territory in the North, 1861–1864." Vol. 41 (1963): 286–98. A look at what was happening to the pro-Union Indians in Kansas.

Fischer, LeRoy H., and Jerry Gill. "Confederate Indian Forces Outside of Indian Territory." Vol. 46 (1968): 249–84.

Fischer, LeRoy H., and Lary C. Rampp. "Quantrill's Civil War Operations in Indian Territory." Vol. 46 (1968): 155–81. Two of the leading scholars team up to picture the bushwhacking aspect of the war in Indian Territory.

Fischer, LeRoy H., and William L. McMurry. "Confederate Refugees from Indian Territory." Vol. 57 (1979–80): 451–62. A reliable version of what was happening to the homeless and destitute families of the Confederate Indians.

Franks, Kenny A. "An Analysis of the Confederate Treaties with the Five Civilized Tribes." Vol. 50 (1972–73): 458–73.

_____. "The Implementation of the Confederate Treaties with the Five Civilized Tribes." Vol. 51 (1973): 21–33. This and the preceding citation are concise accounts of the Confederate-Indian treaties and how they worked in practice.

Franzmann, Tom. "The Final Campaign: The Confederate Offensive of 1864." Vol. 63 (1985): 266–79. An account of the last year of the war in Indian Territory, very complimentary of Maxey.

Halliburton, Janet. "Black Slavery in the Creek Nation." Vol. 56. (1978): 298–314.

Halliburton, R., Jr. "Black Slavery among the Cherokees." Vol. 52 (1974–75): 483–96. This and the preceding article give brief pictures of slavery in two of the Indian nations.

Hancock, Marvin J. "The Second Battle of Cabin Creek, 1864." Vol. 39 (1961–62): 414–26. A more or less standard version of the Confederate million–dollar wagon raid in September 1864.

Heath, Gary N. "The First Federal Invasion of Indian Territory." Vol. 44 (1966–67): 409–19. An account of the unsuccessful Union attempt to win back the Indian Territory in 1862.

Hood, Fred. "Twilight of the Confederacy in Indian Territory." Vol. 41 (1963–64): 425–41. What was happening in the Indian Territory as the war wound toward a close.

Moore, Jessie Randolph. "The Five Great Indian Nations." Vol. 29 (1951): 324–36. A general description of the major tribes of the Indian Territory.

Morton, Ohland. "Confederate Government Relations with the Five
   Civilized Tribes." Vol. 31 (1953): 189–204, 299–322. A picture of
   a partnership that sometimes worked and sometimes didn't.
Shirk, George H. "The Place of Indian Territory in the Command
   Structure of the Civil War." Vol. 45 (1967–68): 464–71. An
   account of how the Confederate Indians fit into the overall
   Confederate structure in the Trans-Mississippi West.
Trickett, Dean. "The Civil War in the Indian Territory." Vol. 17
   (1939): 315–27, 401–12; Vol. 18 (1940): 142–53, 266–80;
   Vol. 19 (1941): 55–69, 381–96. A very valuable account.
   Unfortunately, despite a notice it will be continued, it
   unaccountably ends before the Maxey era begins.
Willey, William J. "The Second Federal Invasion of Indian Territory."
   Vol. 44 (1966–67): 420–30. An account of the successful Union
   effort that wrested back control of a large part of the Indian
   Territory in 1863.
Wright, Muriel H. "General Douglas H. Cooper, C.S.A." Vol. 32
   (1954): 142–84. A good portrait of Maxey's ambitious rival.
Wright, Muriel H., and Leroy H. Fischer. "Civil War Sites in
   Oklahoma." Vol 44 (1966): 158–215. Two of the leading scholars
   of the Confederate Indians team up to revisit the main Civil War
   sites of the Indian Territory.
Dale, Edward Everett. "The Cherokees in the Confederacy."
   Journal of Southern History 13 (May 1947): 159–85. A very
   good rundown of the Cherokees in the Civil War by one of
   the leading scholars of the subject.
Dale, Edward Everett, and Gaston Litton, eds. *Cherokee
   Cavaliers: Forty Years of Cherokee History as Told in the
   Correspondence of the Ridge-Watie-Boudinot Family.*
   Norman: University of Oklahoma Press, 1939. A sampling of
   letters by some of the major Cherokee leaders, spanning the
   antebellum and postbellum as well as the Civil War years.
Debo, Angie. "Southern Refugees of the Cherokee Nation."
   Southwestern Historical Quarterly 35 (April 1932): 255–66.
   An excellent short rundown on the Cherokee refugees in
   1863–64.

Fischer, LeRoy H., ed. *The Civil War in Indian Territory.* Los Angeles: Lorrin L. Morrison, 1974. An excellent anthology of the most important aspects of the Civil War in Indian Territory, including an essay on Sam Bell Maxey.

Geise, William Royston. "The Confederate Military Forces in the Trans-Mississippi West, 1861–1865." PhD. dissertation, University of Texas, 1974. A useful accounting, although not readily accessible.

Gibson, Arrell M. *The Oklahoma Story.* Norman: University of Oklahoma Press, 1978. A very useful and widely available short history of Oklahoma, with several chapters on the state when it was Indian Territory.

Gracy, David B., II., ed. *Maxey's Texas.* Austin, TX: Pemberton Press, 1965. A work of Texas history by Sam Bell Maxey. It includes an excellent biographical sketch of Maxey by the editor.

Grayson, George Washington. *A Creek Warrior for the Confederacy: The Autobiography of Chief G. W. Grayson.* Edited by W. David Baird. Norman: University of Oklahoma Press, 1988. A lively, interesting, often humorous autobiographical account by a young captain destined one day to became chief of the Creek Nation.

Horton, Louise. *Samuel Bell Maxey: A Biography.* Austin: University of Texas Press, 1974. The only comprehensive, book-length biography of Sam Bell Maxey, the standard work. Two articles by Horton on Maxey are also useful: "General Sam Bell Maxey: His Defense of North Texas and the Indian Territory." *Southwestern Historical Quarterly* 74 (1971): 507–24; and "General Samuel Bell Maxey Prepares for the Invasion of Kentucky, Fall 1862." *Register of the Kentucky Historical Society* 79 (1981): 122–35.

Kerby, Robert Lee. *Kirby Smith's Confederacy: The Trans-Mississippi South, 1863–1865.* New York: Columbia University Press, 1972. An excellent work on the Trans-Mississippi West under Edmund Kirby Smith.

Lightfoot, Henry. *In Memoriam: Sam Bell Maxey*. Paris, TX: Privately printed, 1896. An affectionate short memorial to Sam Bell Maxey, including an address and remarks delivered at his funeral by two ministers. Lightfoot, Maxey's son-in-law, also wrote an equally affectionate, longer biographical sketch of his father-in-law in the form of an obituary: "Samuel B. Maxey." In *Twenty-seventh Annual Reunion of the Association of the Graduates of the United States Military Academy, at West Point, New York, June 11th, 1896*. Saginaw, MI: Seemann & Peters, 1896.

Maxey, Sam Bell. Papers. Texas State Archives, Austin, TX.; and Papers. Thomas Gilcrease Institute of American History and Art, Tulsa, OK. These two collections of Maxey's papers are extremely useful, but not easily accessible. Much of his official correspondence found in these papers is more readily available in the Official Records of the Union and Confederate Armies (see below). However, his personal letters to his wife, found largely in the Gilcrease collection, have not been published.

Monaghan, Jay. *Civil War on the Western Border, 1854–1865*. Boston: Little, Brown, 1955. The standard work on the Civil War in the West. It includes some excellent, lively material on the Confederate Indians.

Neville, A. W. *The History of Lamar County (Texas)*. Paris, TX: North Texas Publishing Co., 1937. For those who want to read a history of Maxey's home town of Paris, in Lamar County, Texas.

Nunn, William Curtis, ed. *Ten More Texans in Gray*. Hillsboro, TX: Hill Junior College Press, 1980. Ten short biographies of leading Texas Confederate generals, including Maxey. It is the sequel to a first volume published earlier and titled, *Ten Texans in Gray*.

Rampp, Lary C., and Donald L. Rampp. *The Civil War in Indian Territory*. Austin, TX: Presidial Press, 1975. One of the best reasonably recent accounts of the war in the Indian Territory.

Rampp, Lary C. "Confederate Indian Sinking of the *J.R. Williams.*" *Journal of the West* 11 (1972): 43–50. An excellent account of this important raid lead by Stand Watie in June 1864.

U.S. War Department. *The War of the Rebellion: A Compilation of the Official Records of the Union and Confederate Armies.* 70 vols. in 128 parts. 1880–1901. Reprint. Harrisburg, PA: Historical Times, 1985. These invaluable volumes include important material on Sam Bell Maxey and the Confederate Indians. It includes battle reports and correspondence, scattered through several volumes of Series 1. See in particular vol. 22, part 2; vol. 34, parts 1–4; vol. 41, parts 1–4; vol. 48, parts 1, 2; vol. 53.

Wright, Muriel H. *A Guide to the Indian Tribes of Oklahoma.* Norman: University of Oklahoma Press, 1986. A standard general work on the tribes of the Indian Territory by a foremost scholar.

PHOTO CREDITS

We acknowledge the cooperation of the United States Army Military History Institute, Carlisle Barracks, Pennsylvania, for photographs of Nathaniel Banks, Douglas Cooper, Jefferson Davis, Thomas J. Jackson, Sam Bell Maxey, John Sappington Marmaduke, Albert Pike, Sterling Price, Edmund Kirby Smith, Frederick Steele, Stand Watie, a Union wagon train, and Union Indian soldiers.

We are grateful to the Harold B. Simpson Confederate Research Center, Hillsboro, Texas, for permission to reproduce photographs of Richard Gano, Henry E. McCulloch, and William Steele.

For pictures of Marilda Maxey and Sam Bell Maxey we thank the Archives Division, Texas State Library, Austin, Texas.

INDEX